1976

This book may be kept

FOURTEEN DAYS

EXPERIENTIAL LEARNING

An Effective Teaching Program
for Elementary Schools

EXPERIENTIAL LEARNING

Muriel Schoenbrun Karlin

Parker Publishing Co., Inc.

An Effective Teaching Program for Elementary Schools

and Regina Berger

West Nyack, New York

Experiential Learning:
An Effective Teaching Program
for Elementary Schools

by

Muriel Schoenbrun Karlin
and
Regina Berger

© 1971, BY
PARKER PUBLISHING CO., INC.
West Nyack, N.Y.

LIBRARY OF CONGRESS
CATALOG CARD NUMBER: 78-129305

PRINTED IN THE UNITED STATES OF AMERICA
ISBN-0-13-294744-7
B & P

We dedicate this book to our colleagues, who remain in the classroom despite the ever increasing challenge and the sometimes discouraging variety of problems they encounter daily. This book is dedicated, too, to the children of every race, creed, color, or financial standing whom they teach. May it serve to draw both teachers and children together in a deeper understanding and love for each other.

The authors' previous book ....

Successful Methods for Teaching the Slow Learner
Parker Publishing Co., Inc., West Nyack, N.Y.

Stimulating Thought and Action in Children

The purpose of this book is to suggest a variety of techniques and meaningful experiences that will cause your children to take a more active role in the learning process. We believe your role will become more intellectually challenging as you experiment with these methods; some of them tried and true, others newer to the educational scene. Because of the physical and intellectual activity involved, on the part of the children, we feel you will find your discipline problems reduced, for activity precludes boredom, and it is boredom which causes much disruptive behavior. Your children will have interesting stories and events to tell their families, thereby building their self-esteem, and the materials you are teaching will be retained far longer as a result of your efforts to teach by giving the children learning experiences.

Experiential learning as a method implies far more than the possibility of learning by experience, particularly insofar as you, the teacher, are concerned. It is your task to offer to your students specific situations, and specific stimuli, and it is the reactions to these stimuli which make the learning experiential. The lecture method, for example, rarely offers stimulation unless the lecturer is a superlative craftsman. The teacher who does most of the talking in her classroom usually causes little intellectual activity. But the person who supplies ideas or instruction, or who initiates thought, causes reactions in the minds of the children. Even the simple device of questioning awakens far more mental activity than listening. Watching a film becomes an experience if the teacher stops it before the end, and asks the class, "How do you think this film will end? On what do you base your conclusion?" Taking a class into the basement of your school and showing the youngsters how the heating system works is far more stimulating than a discussion, in the classroom,

7

of boilers and furnaces. Far too often notes are put on the blackboard for the pupils to copy—and then to discuss. What happens to their curiosity? They are frequently thinking of everything but the lesson in front of them. In using the experiential learning method, the teacher is involved in finding a multitude of stimuli, of all kinds, to catch the interest of every child—and, above all, to cause him to react intellectually.

Scarcely a day goes by without a child stopping one of the authors and asking, "Do you have any work for me to do?" The work the child is seeking consists of mimeographing or stapling, of running errands or counting out notices. Fascinating? Hardly—but widely sought after, nevertheless. Why should children want such assignments? Simply because this type of work offers them satisfaction. We feel that work in the classroom must involve thought, action, and physical expression, and we will suggest a great many activities which can be done with any group, to give them the feeling they are actually working. These are activities which will cause the children to respond to intellectual stimulation, and help them experience emotional satisfaction when they have completed their tasks.

Healthy children have a great deal of energy and need activities which will utilize this energy in constructive fashion. Many children, because they have relatively short attention spans, become bored very quickly. A bored child often becomes disruptive. We can do a great deal to make education more effective for these boys and girls if we prevent ennui by giving them meaningful experiences; especially if these experiences occupy them physically as well as intellectually.

There is a great deal of stimulation from sources such as television. The child of today is far, far more sophisticated than the child of even ten years ago. He has seen pictures of the earth as it is viewed from the moon and has been an observer of the battlefield. Is not some of the work given to him in school pallid by comparison? Yet if we give him challenging experiences, if we make his schoolwork vital, if we can utilize the communications media, we can make our classrooms far more exciting, interesting places in which to be.

As teachers, we want to cover a great deal of material with our children. We seek to expand their horizons, to show them the myriad of wonders available in the world around them. And we can do this far more effectively if they experience these wonders rather than if they read or are told about them. We can discuss the shortage of food in the world—and then grow plants in water via the process called hydroponics. Which is more effective—the discussion or the discussion followed by the experience? Reading is a source of great knowledge, and we believe every child must learn to read, but it is not necessarily the only source. Lecturing, particularly to the young child, is probably even less effective. Learning by doing is more far reaching, and is retained much longer than learning by listening or by reading.

All human beings have many psychological needs. As teachers, we are often able to fulfill some of these for our children. For example, everyone needs to experience feelings of satisfaction and achievement. You can supply activities to insure this. Through specific classroom activities such as debates, competitions, or "buzz" sessions, you can make each child feel he belongs, that he is a member of the group.

Most of the techniques, we must stress, should be adapted to fit the needs of your children. Some are basic, but with thought may be made suitable for the junior high school curriculum. We mention a nature walk. For young children, discovering the plants and animals in their immediate surroundings is adequate—and can prove exciting. Ask them, "How many different kinds of living things do you think we will see on our walk?" They will usually guess far fewer than they will actually find, even on the city streets. If you get excited about the variety, so will they. Older students can study the effect of environment on these living things. One might discuss, in this connection, field mice and rabbits, or rats and the need for covered garbage pails. For the upper grades, pollution of the air, of water, and of the land should be added to the environmental study; all of this is tied into the nature walk.

We believe that, by experiential learning, your children will be more satisfied, and their thought processes stimulated. We think that when you apply this program you will find them growing intellectually, participating more, and enjoying the work you put before them as they never have before.

MURIEL SCHOENBRUN KARLIN
REGINA BERGER

ACKNOWLEDGMENTS

We wish to thank the following persons, who have so graciously been of assistance to us:

Mr. Maurice Wollin, Superintendent, District 30, Staten Island.

Mr. Norman H. Harris, Principal, Anning S. Prall Junior High School, Staten Island.

Mrs. Helen R. Harris, Educational and Vocational Counselor, Public School 82, New York, N. Y.

Superintendent Jerome Kovalcik, Office of Education Information Services and Public Relations, Board of Education, City of New York.

Photographers John Kane and John Fulner, Official Photographers for the Board of Education, City of New York.

Mrs. Mary Davies, Public School 39, Staten Island, who so painstakingly prepared our manuscript.

Dr. Leonard Karlin and Mr. Henry Karlin for their careful proofreading of the manuscript, and Miss Lisa Karlin for her photographs.

Mr. Paul Dick, Supervisor of Art, District 30, Staten Island.

Mrs. Thelma Lieberman, Teacher, Anning S. Prall Junior High School, Staten Island.

Our colleagues who have suggested ideas and methods, many of which we eagerly recorded in these pages.

M. S. K.
R. B.

Contents

14

culturation ... Word games ... "Let's tape that!"
... Signs ... Playlets ... Vocabulary bees ... Foreign language picture dictionaries ... Translations ... Let's take a trip ... Using the art of the nation ... Newspapers and magazines ... Class compositions ... Making your foreign language a family affair ... Parlez-vous francais? ... Meet Cantinflas ... Publishing a foreign language magazine ... Poster fun ... Que hora es? ... My day.

Art: Relate the child's experiences in school with his life outside ... Develop tastes for music and art ... Getting children to create ... Creating work in the style of other civilizations, other nations . . . Modeling . . . Research, then create ... Murals ... Integrating art with other subjects ... Trips ... It's a mod, mod world ... Stage sets ... Montages and collages ... Making greeting cards ... Science fiction ... Responding to music with art ... Posters ... Trips to museums and galleries ... Drawing children in the class.

Music: Choose songs the children know and like, and then progress to others ... Encourage the use of instruments in your class ... Reading music ... Arrange performances for all of the children ... Introduce the music of the East ... Using props to motivate music lessons ... Link music with social studies ... Holiday music.

Health Education: Encourage participation ... Field days ... Plays or dances to music ... Introduce rhythms and dancing ... Modern and interpretive dance . . . Exhibitions of skill . . . Square dancing.

Teaching by example ... Arranging projects ... Teaching the history of minority groups ... Dis-

cussing brotherhood openly ... Decorating the classroom with sayings ... Class library ... Panel discussions ... Assembly programs ... Fighting bigotry ... Our own reactions ... Personality clashes or prejudice ... Sensitivity to almost hidden prejudices ... Suggested readings for the teacher ... Handling the bigoted child ... Intellectual discrimination.

Questioning provides an intellectual give-and-take ... Developing the art ... Keep the questioning moving rapidly ... Relating questioning to the children's lives ... Dramatize your questions ... Stimulating your children's natural curiosity ... Testing.

· · · 1 · · ·

How to Use the Experiential Learning Program

Experiential learning differs from conventional teaching in several extremely important aspects. It stresses giving the children a multiplicity of experiences, rather than instructing them by lecturing or reading. It involves stimulating them to thought and action. It emphasizes learnings and activities which are relevant to the child's life. In other words, it is the kind of teaching which is in tune with today because it "jumps." No sedentary program this; it is just the opposite—vital, moving, living, and breathing—and it is made so by the reactions of the children.

As you read the pages which follow, you will find many techniques which will help you get your youngsters into activities and into action. You will find the stimuli, the motivational devices, the methods to do this. But, you ask, "Why should I use these methods; why can't I teach while the children sit and learn?" The answer to that question is simply "You can make them sit, but you can't make them learn." You can't demand interest, you must entice it. You cannot mandate creativity, you have to nurture it. You cannot drill a hole and pour knowledge into the cranium. In the words of an old adage: "You can lead a horse to water, but you can't make him drink." We believe that, by using the methods we have grouped into "experiential learning," you will at least encourage your children to drink of the font of knowledge, and react to the stimulation you offer them.

What benefits will you, the teacher, gain by your use of this program? We believe you will find your own interest increasing and your own enthusiasm building, for the accent here is on creativity—your's and the children's. If the experiences you offer to your children are really vital and involve them, we feel you will discover, too, that your discipline problems will be diminished. It may appear to you that the

21

techniques we suggest cause an undesirable hum in the classroom, but this sound is desirable, for it is an indication of intellectual activity which has been stirred up, the reaction to stimuli you have brought to the children. We honestly believe you will become a better teacher as a result of this kind of teaching, because you will be encouraging your pupils to work—intellectually and often physically, as well.

As you use it, you will find this program is extremely flexible—because it may be used alone, or in conjunction with other teaching techniques. You will note, too, that it has built-in motivation, and that the children will often learn preparatory material as well, because they require skills to participate in certain activities.

Your first task is establishing a climate for experiential learning, stressing self-control and responsibility. You must remain the figure of authority in the classroom, guiding and supervising. We will try to show you how to do this, in this chapter. You begin by emphasizing the need for soft voices and low tones, and insist upon this. Encourage cooperation, avoiding hostility at all costs, but do not accept misbehavior of any kind. Involve the children in your planning, and select their experiences with care—so that they are motivational in and of themselves. By approbation rather than criticism, by fostering cooperation, and by equitable distribution of work, you will encourage the children to greater achievement.

UNDERSTANDING THE EXPERIENTIAL LEARNING PROGRAM

Are you a member of a generation which had to sit for hours, hands folded, listening to your teacher? Perhaps the class had been uncooperative, and then sometimes the children were required to place their hands behind their backs. How detrimental this must have been, not only to the mind, but even to the body, for both mind and body seek expression in action! Is it not then imperative that we cooperate with nature when she demands this outpouring of activity? Walt Whitman refers to these as "primal sanities." We can see the manifestation of this in every normal, healthy child.

Have you observed adults doodling, tapping their feet, humming, whistling, or pacing, and so finding an outlet for their energies? How much more difficult it is for a child to sit still, a child whose impulses impel him to run and jump, to play and be free. These impulses are nature's mandates that activities of mind and body be furnished to promote the good health and well-being of the child. The experiential learning program takes full cognizance of this deep need for intellectual and physical activity.

There are other benefits which will accrue to both teacher and pupil by employing methods devoted to experiential learning, rather than the hackneyed, old-fashioned lecture methods which are so often dull and enervating.

Why try to make your lessons experiential?

1. You, yourself, will find a challenge, a new source of intellectual stimulation. Your eyes and ears will open to techniques, to games and new devices. You may see a television quiz show and ask yourself, as many successful teachers do, "How can I use that format to suit my classes?" You may hear an actor read a selection, or act in a play, and say to yourself, "That's just the thing for my children."

2. If you offer your youngsters learning experiences which are different, unusual, and (hopefully) exciting, you will have far less difficulty controlling their behavior. Young people want new experiences. We see this in their entire modus operandi. Teenagers' music, their light shows, their clothing, their favorite television programs—all of this reflects a search for the new. Remember, even though a technique may have been used thousands of times before, if your children have never been exposed to it, it is brand new to them. If you supply stimuli to youngsters, certainly much tamer, but new nevertheless, you will encounter a different attitude on their part. I recall hearing one girl say to another as they entered a classroom, "I wonder what's on for today." From the manner in which it was said, one could tell it was a compliment to the teacher. What actually was "on," in this language arts class, was this: As the teacher was discussing one of the vocabulary words which was part of the "warm-up," a boy ran into the room, shouting, "I'm looking for my lunch." He proceeded to look in each desk. He then shouted gleefully, "I found it," and ran out again. He was not polite, he did not ask permission, and his behavior was very strange.

Then the teacher asked each student in the class to write a paragraph describing the incident, as if for a newspaper article. These were read to the class. The lesson was in recording observations, and the most interesting outcome was that not one observer noted the single, but most critical, detail—that the young man carried no package out of the room, that the entire performance had been staged. Try this lesson with your class—it stimulates thought, and it's lots of fun.

Discipline problems come from a number of causes, of which boredom may be considered "Public Enemy Number One." One substitute teacher we know enters a classroom and tells the children, "I have a lesson prepared which you will find is valuable as far as your future is concerned. I promise you will be interested—but you must give me a chance—five minutes of complete cooperation, in which I can begin it with you. If you don't agree after that, then we can decide what we shall do instead." Ninety-nine per cent of the time they forget everything else during that lesson. It is on cancer and cancer research, in terms of themselves and their lives, and is truly spellbinding. The young lady had been a laboratory technician working on a project involving viruses suspected of causing cancer. She decided she would like to try teaching, and used her knowledge of her subject to work up the best possible lesson she could. The children were not bored for one single second. Consequently, there were no discipline problems.

Remember, young people have, for the most part, a huge amount of physical energy. They cannot sit still doing nothing. If you get them interested, you can easily channel this energy into worthwhile activities. For example, they love to discuss problems—and holding "buzz" sessions is an excellent device for doing this. The class is divided into groups of five or six children, who talk among themselves, and then one of each group gives the results to the rest of the class. They may talk about books they have been assigned, plays they have seen in the auditorium, problems at home, or difficulties in school. The point is to give them the opportunity for self-expression, and a sense of freedom of thought.

3. At dinnertime, among families throughout the United States, the question is usually asked, "What did you do in school today?" How often is the answer, "Nothing!"? Don't you feel, as we do, that we should supply the answer—by giving children experiences they are anxious to talk about? Our youngsters can gain status in their family constellation if they are able to volunteer information—such as facts not known to the others, anecdotes—and above all, stories of things which happened to them.

4. Your teaching will be memorable. Search your memory. You will find that you, yourself, remember those teachers who were interesting—who stimulated your thinking. You must, of course, cover the curriculum—but in teaching with the goal of giving experiential lessons, you can include all of the prescribed material, and far, far more. Children can learn a prodigious amount if it is presented well. They will not remember it all (who ever does?), but they will retain

24

a great deal—if you present it, or if it is "discovered" by your children, themselves. Reading is, of course, one of the major tools of teaching, and, while it is certainly an important one, we believe it must not be used to the exclusion of any of the others.

There are experiences included in this book which are really quite conventional. Others, you will agree, are out of the ordinary. Choose those fitting the needs of your classes and yourself. But, far more important, start thinking of your own unusual approaches. Don't be afraid to experiment. Certain methods, you will discover, fit right into the work you are doing, into your curriculum or syllabus. Please try them. However, when you find a technique which intrigues you, and is not specifically related to any area, use it anyway for enrichment. Don't be afraid to digress, because you are working with the underlying philosophy that young minds are like sponges, and that we must give them an ocean to sop up.

HOW IS THE EXPERIENTIAL PROGRAM USED?

This program may be used either alone or in conjunction with other methods. There are, for example, certain concepts which it is extremely difficult to teach experientially, but which must be taught. You may wish to use the developmental method in teaching them. However, it is suggested that, whenever and wherever you possibly can, you follow up with the experiential method. For instance, after a developmental reading lesson, try having the children dramatize the material—providing it lends itself to dramatization. Narrative poems or plays are excellent for this purpose, and short stories can be handled in this way too. What could be more exciting than having the children read Sidney Carton's famous words, "Tis a far, far better thing I do. . . ."

In teaching grammar, create games. Use a charade type to act out verbs. Each child dramatizes the word, and the class has to guess what it is. You may wish to try this with adjectives and adverbs as well.

TEACHING SKILLS TO PREPARE FOR EXPERIENCES

The experiential learning program involves using a great many activities and projects. It is often necessary to teach the skills required to participate in the activities or to complete the projects. If a child wishes to contribute to a class book or the school newspaper, you may have to work with him on writing skills, teaching him the rudiments of writing. However, by helping the youngster see the reason you are teaching the skill to him, you will make him more receptive to your teaching. Children will really study the multiplication table to participate in a competition (similar to the old spelling bee variety.) They will ask for assistance in reading if they must read instructions to build a radio or fix a carburetor. If they realize there is a genuine need, and if they feel it themselves, you will, without doubt, experience far greater ease in teaching them. We are familiar with the case of a boy who could not read before, but learned in the sixth grade because he became fascinated with cars, and sought to read the manuals giving instruction in automobile construction.

Is there anyone who does not, at some time in his life, need to write a business letter? You can set up a situation, having your class write for something—free tickets to a television or radio broadcast, printed materials for reports, an interview, or an invitation to a famous person to visit the school. Then you are able to include the skill of writing such a letter. If the children are given an experience—particularly one which interests them—they will learn remarkably quickly. You may even have them write to celebrities for autographs. One ten-year-old we know was thrilled to receive a letter from Mrs. Indira Gandhi in response to one she had written to this lady prime minister of India.

What is more stimulating than purposeful activity? Your children realize this, and are willing to cooperate with you in preparing themselves for these activities. For example, if a child is to take part in a dramatization of the story of King Henry VIII, he will not be averse to hunting up the historical facts he will need to make the rendition praiseworthy. If a girl wishes to make a dress for herself, she will be motivated to learn to read the instructions associated with the pattern. If a boy wants to construct a Van de Graaff generator, he will be anxious to read and comprehend the directions necessary to build it. If a child wishes to get tickets for a performance of a sports event, a play, or a movie, he may write requesting reduced admission rates.

HOW TO ESTABLISH A CLIMATE FOR THE EXPERIENTIAL TEACHING PROGRAM

In following the experiential program, a dead silence is taboo. It is to be expected that there is a certain amount of wholesome sound, born of interest and enthusiasm in the activity. If yours is the type of personality that seeks an absolutely silent classroom, try to realize that this is not possible in the experiential situation. When you are aware of the fact that sound does not signify lack of control, and that it is far more important to train the children in self-control, and in using soft rather than loud voices, you will be better able to relax and enjoy your work. The experiential teaching program is one you should enjoy. You will not be constantly "on stage," trying to attract the children's attention. You will not have to hold them spellbound. Your activities do these things for you. Are you putting on a play? Then your lesson cannot be lifeless, nor the rendition spiritless. This, however, surely does not imply uncontrolled noise, which would destroy the benefits derived from the program.

With the goal of self-directed, self-motivated work—work which is enjoyed by every child in the class—we suggest you carefully consider each of the following concepts:

1. Establish from the very beginning of the program, the need for each child to speak in a soft, well-modulated voice. Regular speech is too loud, for there are often many voices to be heard. Do not permit the noise level to disturb anyone in the class. In the beginning the boys and girls will be amenable, but as the term progresses they will probably need to be reminded. If so, be sure to keep reminding them.

2. Do not react with hostility if you find the children are getting a bit loud. Instead, speak to those who are causing the problem, asking them for their cooperation. Use positive psychology—namely, telling the children: "I know everyone wishes to work. Some of you may have forgotten and raised your voices. I must remind you this is impossible, because it disturbs everyone else." If you are hostile, they will be too, for hostility breeds anger, and hostility in return. This is to be avoided at all costs. A child will react far better to an explanation than an argument, a gesture rather than a shout.

3. Do not tolerate for one minute uncontrollable shouting or screaming. The children must be taught to work quietly and control their natural enthusiasm. If your activities are pleasant and interesting enough, your children will cooperate because they are involved, and because they will seek other similar intriguing experiential lessons.

4. Involve the children in the experiential lessons you are planning. If they do not cooperate, warn them that these will be withdrawn, and if need be, take them away temporarily. Never threaten to do something you cannot follow through on. The children will soon

27

Official Photograph—Board of Education, City of N.Y.

Figure 1-1. Chinese New Year's celebration.

learn whether their teacher is sincere or not. If you make a threat and forget it, you will be fair game, for they will realize that you are bluffing. Do not risk your reputation or your rapport with them.

5. Choose activities which both you and the children enjoy. In this way, you will develop in them a taste for learning. They will not come to school reluctantly. We witnessed one class arriving at school daily about an hour before they were scheduled to do so. They were doing a study of ghosts and the supernatural. The interest had been kindled when the class read portions of Dickens' *Christmas Carol.* Their teacher had asked, "How many of you believe in ghosts?" A lively discussion ensued. It was brought out that two girls in another class had seen flashing lights, which had led them to a hiding place where they found several thousand dollars. These young ladies were invited to tell of their experiences, so that the class heard the details firsthand. From ghosts, the discussion went to Ouija boards,

to seances, and to mediums. A play was produced, a debate held, and the local newspaper sent a reporter to meet with the class. She subsequently wrote a feature story for "National Ghost Week." But, most of all, can you imagine the excitement generated and the interest and enthusiasm? Try a similar subject with your classes—and from the story you have them read, progress to having them tell of their experiences with the supernatural (or with what they believe to be the supernatural).

Treasure hunts were a very successful dinner party diversion, and are even more fun for the children. Playlets composed on the spot are vital, and will enthrall the youngsters. (That was the method used to develop the play on ghosts, mentioned previously.) Pursue the children's interests, follow their leads, and while they will need supervision and guidance, they will require far, far fewer disciplinary measures. Become absorbed in their world and in their viewpoints. You will be fascinated and enriched as a result. An open mind and an open heart on your part will invite their confidences, which the young are so eager to divulge. This emotional catharsis is salutary for them. As Hamlet suggests, "Let them unpack their hearts with words." Even though considerable leeway must be given to the children during the experiential lesson, the teacher never ceases to be the figure of authority, although no psychological oppression is ever exercised by him. This means you will never permit a child to annoy or bully other children, to waste his time or the time of the class, or to shout or disrupt the proceedings in any way. However, you wish to maintain a climate of freedom of expression which will generate the ideas and beliefs of all of the children, and stimulate them intellectually and creatively.

Since children do not work at exactly the same rate, have on hand work for them to do when they have finished the class assignment. If it is a play, some of the boys and girls may be making programs or drawing posters. Others may be making scenery. Whatever they are doing, be sure there is some work for each child, at all times.

You may wish to use a method we found eminently successful. Each child had a library book (from the class or the public library) in his desk. He read it when he had finished his class assignment. Or there were magazines on racks at the back of the room, which were borrowed when the youngsters had finished their work. If your school has a literary magazine, make copies from previous years available in this way. Children particularly enjoy reading material written by their peers.

Official Photograph—Board of Education, City of N.Y.

Figure 1-2

6. Encourage the children, praise their work, and display it as often as possible. Each youngster's work should be included—even if this requires maneuvering on your part. It is essential that every boy and girl feel he belongs, and is a member in good standing of the group (the class). He must feel he has successfully completed his work in school. Every youngster needs this encouragement, this self-confidence, this feeling that he is contributing. Each must be helped in the greatest measure to develop his concept of self-worth.

There are children who rarely, if ever, experience these feelings. Call them slow learners, disadvantaged, or what you will, their pattern in school has been one of constant failure, constant frustration. We must devote our time and attention to these children, especially. They are the ones who will benefit in large measure from the experiential learning program, for you can and must structure situations, projects, and activities in which they will be successful. You will find many in the pages of this book. For example, an excellent device to accomplish this goal (useful on every grade level) is having each child compile his own scrapbook. Allow the children to select their own topics, topics in which they are interested. This is extremely important, if the book is to have meaning for them. They are to gather pictures from newspapers and magazines relative to their subject. Current events and sports come to mind immediately, but other topics are equally good. Below each photograph to be placed in the scrapbook, the child should be instructed to write a comment. For very young children it may be but a few words (depending on their abilities.) For third graders a sentence would be adequate. With older children, through junior high school, a paragraph discussing the photo should be required.

Encourage the children to gather as much material as they can. It is sometimes necessary for the teacher to supply outdated magazines for this purpose. Ask your children to bring them into school and seek contributions from other teachers and classes as well. Discarded textbooks may be used and are often available for the asking. Construction paper makes an excellent book, into which the materials can be pasted, if the children cannot afford to purchase one. Make sure each boy and girl understands he or she will be given credit for making the book, and that, when they have been completed, the scrapbooks are placed on display in the classroom—not just the best ones, but every single book. This is an activity in which every child can be successful, and we have found it to be an exceptionally good one. One young man, for example, brought in a book with well over 100 photographs. His paragraphs were not very long, but his book became the talk of the school. He had wisely used photographs from a sports magazine, which were truly magnificent. He was vitally interested in his topic, and the resulting book was a labor of love.

7. Foster cooperation among the children by your selection of activities and projects. The experiential learning program truly prepares the youngsters for their future lives, for, in many respects, they are given the opportunity to learn the very important lesson of getting along with and working with others. Always keep in mind the concept—and teach it, too—that each child is part of a group; he must work not only for himself, but also for the good of the entire group.

Encourage the children to help one another and work toward common goals, when these are established. A newspaper is a group effort; whereas, a play might not be so considered. Yet both, of course, are group activities—and it is important that the·children recognize this.

8. A wise distribution of the work involved in any activity is exceedingly important. Favoritism must be studiously avoided, for the children sense it immediately and resent it deeply. Duplicate projects or enlarge upon them, but do not slight any child. Give each an equal opportunity to participate and learn. The weaker a child's intellectual powers, the more he needs to take part, so that he may benefit spiritually and intellectually. There is too much impoverishment in the outside world! Let us avoid it in our classrooms. The greater a child's need, the greater should be the teacher's wish to fulfill that need.

9. An intrinsic part of the experiential learning program is taking your children on trips. It is a process of bringing to your youngsters as many of the outside resources as you possibly can. Trips to the theatre, to museums, to broadcasting stations, to factories, parks, and National Historic Sites—to any place which will enrich their lives—are most worthwhile. Through these visits, you are able to introduce your boys and girls to new facets of the world which they may never have realized existed. You will find suggestions for trips, as they are related to the various subject areas, in the chapters which follow. We believe their value cannot be overestimated. Unfortunately, many of the children we teach have never gone very far from their immediate environment. An example: we took one class on a trip to a planetarium. Most of the children had been there before with their previous teachers, but they had not seen the program we took them to see. One child, how-

Photo by Sandra De Veau

Figure 1-3. Official photograph, Mystic Seaport, Mystic, Connecticut.

ever, had never even visited the building before, and was particularly ecstatic. The story is noteworthy because of her father's profession; he is a science teacher.

STARTING ON YOUR OWN EXPERIENTIAL LEARNING PROGRAM

How would you begin your own program, assuming you would like to experiment with this type of teaching?

1. As you plan your lessons, consider each one individually. Try to find an experience you can give to your children, related to the particular topic. Start with one or two subjects, and plan as interesting an experience as you can. Perhaps you would like to try some of the

33

methods you will find outlined in this book. Perhaps you will learn of particularly effective techniques from some of your colleagues. However, find something, some experience, about which you, yourself, get excited, and use that as your initial attempt. Note your children's reactions and use them as a barometer of success.

If you are teaching fractions, what can you have your children divide? A real pie can prove to be far more effective—even if it is portioned into 25ths or 30ths. Then go on to a paper pie, and finally to a diagram on the board.

What about a topic such as immigration? Ah——have your children question their relatives—for eyewitness accounts. You may write to the Federal Government, seeking to borrow the marvelous film which was exhibited at the New York World's Fair, in the United States Pavilion. You may recommend books describing the voyages of many people to America, from Columbus to those who arrived last year.

Even grammar may become experiential, if you select sentences from the children's own compositions, write them on the board, duplicate them, and have the children work on them, themselves, making the necessary corrections, and discussing the reasons for them.

2. Make your desk a veritable treasure-house of do-it-yourself ideas. Jot down any you find, hear, or think of when they come to you. File cards (3 X 5), used for each subject, are convenient and easy to refer to as you write your lesson plans. Discuss and trade ideas with your fellow teachers. You will find you obtain many, many fine ideas in this way.

3. Don't be afraid to experiment. Try out new ideas—the more unusual the better. In one of the author's science classes, fertilizers were being studied. We wish to state right here that this is an experiment which should be done out-of-doors. We tried coffee grounds, eggshells, and the straw which broke the camel's back, ground-up fish bones. The room was warm, sunny—and can you imagine how it smelled?

In every class, not only science, a spirit of experimentation can add to the excitement. Give your students the opportunities to try their wings. If they have seen the wonderful film of Romeo and Juliet, might they not read the balcony scene? Introduce Haiku, and have them write their own poems. Have them answer questions of a "lonely hearts" nature: for example,

"My mother thinks I am too young to go to dances. I am 13. How can I convince her? Don't you think I am old enough?"

Should you use letters of this type to provoke interest, be sure to tie them in with the pupils' lives. A ten-year-old usually is more involved with sports than with social situations, with horses rather than members of the opposite sex.

4. Get ideas from your children. Often they come up with excellent contributions, if given the opportunities to do so. Again drawing from science, we had a fascinating experience as a result of a child's idea. We all know about a leopard's spots, but what about a chameleon? We discovered we could place one of these marvelous little animals on a sheet of green construction paper, and *he would turn green*. When placed on light-brown colored paper, he became that color. Why? A marvelous topic for investigation resulted.

5. Make the world your classroom—the entire world. Plan to take your children on trips. Invite speakers in to talk to them. Show them films and slides. Utilize television and radio programs. Play recordings. Make the walls disappear and allow the only limits to be your imagination, and the imagination of your children. Walk in the park on a snowy day, and think aloud of the weather, and the way in which it affects all of nature—and man. Visit a college with your children, explaining what college actually is. If there is a policeman who can come to speak to them, have him tell your children about his work. Is there a building being built in your neighborhood? Visit the site and take pictures. Then have the children give their impressions—in paint or in words. Use every device you can think of to make them aware, and to open their eyes. Involve them in the fight against hunger—in our own country, and in the world. Get them concerned about pollution —of air, of water, and of land. We are living in times which are fascinating, but of which our children must be made aware. Use every media of communication to bring to them the ever changing universe. To borrow a famous slogan, "Up, up and away...."

Conclusion

Teaching through experiences is stimulating and challenging to both teacher and children. Interest heightens, and discipline problems are usually far less frequent as a result. Since this type of program is very flexible, you may use it as often as you wish but it need not limit or restrict you.

You must, however, set up a structured situation in which such experiences are possible, stressing to the children the need for modulation of voices and their cooperation. Hopefully, you will find they are using their energies constructively and accomplishing much work. They will be interested, for the most part, in activities, if you select those fitting their needs for their particular lives and circumstances.

In constructing your own experiential program, you will find that one activity leads to another. Select some from the variety we offer you and adjust them to meet the needs of your class. If they are poor readers, try having them read comic books. Try to use the most dramatic, the most exciting and enticing in the very beginning, so that you "hook them"— gain their wholehearted support. Get them with you, rather than "agin'" you. If they are apathetic, find something that will shake them up. In using the experiential program, we believe you will find your own tasks easier, more stimulating, and most satisfying, for the creativity involved is health building and soul building, both for you and for the children.

··· **2** ···

How to Make Learning Experiences Exciting in Every Subject Area

We have walked into class after class and been overwhelmed by the feeling of lethargy which pervades the very air. By contrast, we have also entered many classes where the atmosphere is crackling—where we could almost feel the thought waves traveling through the air. In these rooms one cannot immediately discern which are the slow or the bright children, because all of them are caught up in the work going on in the room. We have attempted to analyze the latter classes, in terms of teaching methods and techniques, and we shall introduce a variety of them to you.

Many years ago, a cereal salesman from Battle Creek, Michigan wanted to create interest in his product. He decided to put a little surprise gift, a lagniappe, into each package of dry cereal. Within a decade he was famous, and still is. W. K. Kellogg originated what is known in the trade as "gimmicks." We, too, need to sell our product; we can borrow his idea of giving gifts, of adding something extra. Following the curriculum is fine, but it probably won't make your children love your subject; it is the novel experiences which will. We find, too, that we are in competition with other media at every turn. Television comes to mind immediately, and indeed it is conceivable that it could replace us—for televised lessons may be used to teach subject matter to huge numbers of students. Instead, we must turn it into one of our tools. If we allow ourselves to become stilted and complacent, if we do not give our children experiences, if we do not project our personalities, our warmth and ingenuity, are we not ignoring our most important assets? Teaching machines, too, are available, if all that is sought for children is mere information. Based on sound psychological laws of learning, they offer instant gratification, which can be attractive and at times effective. But inanimate objects can never teach in the manner in which we can—they cannot offer a variety of experiences, and they cannot possibly make learning alive, exciting, and appealing. As teachers, we must be aware, though, of the age in which we live—of electronics, automation, and of an entirely new outlook on life; and we must use this to our children's advantage. If we can't "beat 'em," we have to join them.

You will have to find a variety of learning experiences in this chapter, which may be applied to almost any and all subject areas. Treasure hunts are suggested; trips to the theatre (but with purpose); publishing a class magazine or newspaper; debates; overtime work, in the form of bonus assignments; children's contributions; varying of experiences; competitions; making your room an experience in itself; games; plays and playlets; experiments; keeping a notebook; writing on the board; allowing children to teach. Each technique offers your children a valuable learning experience—something in which he actively participates. All are successfully used and worth trying.

SPECIFIC METHODS

Try a Treasure Hunt

Some years ago treasure hunts were party diversions. They are excellent learning experiences, and still fun. The following lists are given to help you create your own, although you may certainly use these if you wish.

For science: 1. *A leaf from a fossil tree. (Have the children try to determine which tree fits the description. It is actually the ginko, and is found in most areas of the country. Check to be sure there is a specimen somewhere near your school.)* 2. *A claw from an arachnoid.* 3. *A sample of a mineral.* 4. *A photograph of an eclipse.* 5. *A blond hair with a black root.*

We would allow about a week to gather these items.

For language arts: 1. *Who said, "The quality of mercy is not strained."?* 2. *Find a picture of the home of the author of Rip Van Winkle.* 3. *Select and copy a poem about a bird and about a mammal.* 4. *Bring in a book with a short story about an insect.* 5. *Look for and bring to school a book about a stargazer who lived long ago.*

For math: 1. *A foreign coin worth less than one penny.* 2. *A ruler divided into centimeters.* 3. *A model of a rhomboid made of card-*

board. 4. A Centigrade thermometer. 5. A graph of current trends of the stock market.

For social studies: 1. An old newspaper (at least five years old.) 2. A copy of John F. Kennedy's Inaugural Address. 3. A description of the sinking of the **Titanic.** 4. A recording of the voice of Franklin D. Roosevelt (available from the public library.) 5. A map of the world at the time of Christopher Columbus.

For students of various foreign languages: 1. A menu in the language of the country, accompanied by an English translation. 2. A song in that language and its translation into English. 3. A travel poster. 4. A novel written in that language. 5. A list of five important places in the capital city, with a short description of each place in the language.

On all of these treasure hunts, point out to the children that the

Official Photograph—Board of Education, City of N.Y

Figure 2-1

local or school librarians will be very good friends. Make many variations "of objects to be found," but, above all, make them fun.

Trips to the Theatre

If professional, college, or even amateur theatres are to be found in your community, utilize their offerings when they are in some way connected with your curriculum, and also for enriching it. Give your classes the background information they need and then tell them why the trip to the theatre is being included in their work; give them assignments to do after they have seen the play—so that the experience is both a learning situation and an entertainment, and so that they will derive as much benefit from it as possible. For example, "Galileo" is often being produced and is excellent for science, social studies, or language arts classes; "Camelot" for the latter two. You might give an assignment to prepare for a discussion based on the following questions:

- What was the attitude toward women at the time of this story? How is it compared with that of today's people?
- What contributions did the main character make to society? To you, personally?
- How is the country in which the play took place different from the United States of today? Would you like to have lived at that time or today? Why?
- What would you have done if you were Galileo? If you were King Arthur? If you were Guinevere?
- What is the difference between a legend and a factual story? Can a legend be based on fact? Who are some of the people who are being made into the living legends of today?

If you wanted to utilize the theatre for a math class, you might work out a unit involving the financial aspects of the production of a particular play—the budget, the expenses—and, as a culmination of the unit, take the class to see the play.

Moving pictures, too, are of value. "A Man for All Seasons," is appropriate for language arts classes and for social studies. Many films can be used to teach history in a far more exciting manner than we are able to teach it in the classroom. Isn't it a good idea to combine the two? Foreign films are available, but be sure you preview them first.

The "Theatre of the Stars" is the title often used by most planetariums. Previewing is important in this area, too, for such shows may be excellent or they may be dreadfully boring. Nevertheless, we feel this is a valuable experience for every child—providing it is a stimulating show. Find the most exciting on the calendar. Beware of presentations about constellations, however, since they are usually not within the children's range of interests or grasp. Eclipses and rockets, as a general rule, are of great interest to children. You are usually able to obtain a listing of the programs for the year, and then you can choose intelligently.

Trips of the kinds mentioned are useful either as motivation or as reward for good behavior. Almost every child enjoys an outing. Have the children carry out all of the business aspects of the trip—collecting money, issuing receipts, and paying the bills. If you believe the majority of the boys and girls can afford to pay for the trip, assign monitors to collect the money. If the cost per child is calculated to be $1.75, have each child bring in $2.00. In this way, you can absorb the expense for the few children who cannot afford to pay their own way. Be sure to tell your children, "We never leave any child at home for lack of funds. Anyone who wishes to go on the trip but cannot pay for it, or who would like to borrow the money, is to see me privately any time during the day. We will make arrangements. We want each and every one of you to go." We have found children generally do not take advantage—that few have asked for special consideration if they did not need it. Indeed, we have received money, long after the day the trip was taken, from grateful mothers whose husbands had finally found work.

If you teach in an area which is financially disadvantaged, we suggest you write to any theatre which has a presentation to which you would like to take your children, asking for special consideration. Very often it will be forthcoming. (We've even obtained free admission and invitations for lunch. Most of the time though, there are relatively inexpensive performances scheduled for school children.) If you cannot get rates which are inexpensive enough, you might consult your Parent Association. There may be a way to raise funds for the outing. Check too, to determine whether there are federal or school funds which may be used for the purpose. The effort you make, you will find, is definitely worthwhile—for the theatre may prove to be a very vital part of your teaching, and may introduce your children to an entirely new, fascinating world.

43

Publish a Class Magazine or a Class Newspaper

This is an extremely useful and valuable way to give children real experience. Discuss your ideas with your children and invite them to make suggestions. By mentioning this early in the year, you are able to start getting contributions of written material. from every one of the children almost immediately. Tell them their work must be of interest to their classmates, and to their parents, who will be reading the publication. Include factual articles and humorous material, too, and novelty items, personal anecdotes, cartoons, comic strips, puzzles, and "Letters to the Editors." When you assign work, to be done either in class or at home, you may link it up to the newspaper, which makes it far more meaningful. In math, for example, your class might enjoy working up a problem sheet. Have the children submit the problems with their solutions. The best are published in a biweekly or monthly publication.

In science, even with a rather uninspiring topic such as plant reproduction, you are able to make the newspaper exciting. The headline might read, "Plants Take Over the Earth! Man Being Pushed Out!" You've guessed it—science fiction, but based on factual knowledge which must appear in the articles.

In social studies, the headline might be "Through the Eyes of the People Living in the Twenty-first Century." Doesn't that give you ideas?

Rexographing or mimeographing the publication makes the "publishing" simple. If a child is able to type the material, allow him to do so. If not, you may seek help from the parents, who, very often, will be more than pleased to assist.

Above all, every child must have the experience of seeing his work in print. This may require much assistance from you—but it is a basic concept of the experiential learning program that each child be able to achieve successfully in school, and that his work must be represented.

Debates

In any subject, debates are an excellent device to bring children out—to give them experiences and get them involved. To prepare for a debate, the children must research their topic thoroughly. Even the slow learners are able to do this—if you pair them with children who are able to read well. If you assign a series of these debates, with adequate time for preparation, each child gets the opportunity to participate and to make his views known. We suggest you act as a consultant yourself.

Your debates may be curriculum oriented or used for enrichment, but, either way, choose topics such as "Old enough to fight, old enough to vote," "Did Lee Harvey Oswald really act alone, or were others involved with him in the murder of President John F. Kennedy?" "Is it morally ethical to transplant the human heart?" You may prefer to phrase this, "Should people be given other people's hearts?" "Installment buying, should you or shouldn't you?" It may be necessary to have some children take the opposite side, play the "devil's advocate," to present both sides of the picture. They will be willing to do this if you instruct them and state to the class: "Jack and Mary are arguing the other side, to make debate possible. This does not reflect the way they actually feel about the issue." It may be a good idea for you to play that role yourself the first time, to show what you mean by "devil's advocate." In science, how would your children react to such topics as "Little green men from Mars—fact or fiction?" "Why is electronic music becoming the music of our era?" In social studies, "Is there really a generation gap?" (With young children it is not nearly as pronounced as with the older groups.) Are you asking if all children—slow or bright—can take part in such debates? Please experiment—we think you may be very pleasantly surprised. Another possible topic—"Should there be school for 11 months per year?" (The teacher is not permitted to overrule the children. We are sure the boys and girls will clamor to vote yes.)

It is possible that you will have to instill confidence in some children in order to get them to participate. It is truly worth your efforts. They will "come to life" if you give them proper guidance. You will find, too, that such activities and experiences bring forth leaders, and we should surely work to develop such leadership qualities in our children.

Overtime Work—Bonus Assignments

In our society we are paid wages for our work, and in many occupations the more time we work, the more money we are able to earn.

Let us translate this experience to our children's lives. By giving bonus assignments, we provide them the opportunity to "work overtime" and therefore improve their grades. These assignments should require some research, on the part of the children, and should be of some significance as far as the topic is concerned. Choose topics of interest so that there is dual motivation. If you say you will give credit for doing the assignment, make sure that the pupil sees exactly what he is getting. If by doing such work, a child can raise himself from a failing grade to a passing one, why not?—or from 70 per cent to 75 per cent, or even from 90 per cent to 95 per cent. Have the children do work which they will be interested in, so that the overtime experience is not an unpleasant one.

You may wish to assign short biographical reports on the brilliant people in your subject area—for example, von Guericke, in science, or Einstein, Jefferson, or da Vinci.

You might choose important, but relatively unknown contributors— Crispus Attucks or Robert Goddard, for instance.

You could introduce topics in which a child might become interested as a result of classwork: science fiction; psychology; mechanics; agriculture. If a child wants to learn more about anything, help him, refer him to good resource materials, and give him credit for it. For example, baking may be related to science as well as home economics, because of the action of baking powder in the baked goods. (The action of carbon dioxide is always an interesting topic. It has many uses.)

When a piece of worthwhile work is handed in, give the child experience in public speaking by having him tell the class about it, in addition to extra credit in terms of his grade. With slow children, you may wish to help them bring their marks up, and you can do this by working with them on each stage of their bonus work, until the project is worthy of the credit you give it.

Pupil Contributions

Encourage children to bring in to class any pictures, articles, or ideas they find interesting for class discussion. Even if your time is limited, it is far better to cram it full than to stretch your lessons. Every child gets satisfaction from such participation.

Children may wish to write for materials which they may show to their classmates. The Public Relations Department of General Electric, Schenectady, New York, or your local telephone company are sources for posters, booklets, and other items which are instructional and interesting. If a child finds a rock or a fossil, a magnet or an Indian bell—if he thinks it worthwhile, allow him to share it with his classmates. By giving extra credit for such things, you encourage such contributions from almost every child.

Give the children experiences of many different varieties. If you are teaching a lesson on superstitions, have the children actually walk under a ladder or open an umbrella in the classroom. If you wish to have the braver ones break a mirror to further motivate the lesson, for safety's sake wrap it in paper toweling. In social studies classes conduct opinion polls, following the same procedures Harris or Gallup do. If you have your language arts classes write poems, allow the children to set them to music. Undoubtedly there is either a pianist or a guitarist in the class. Even famous poems may be sung as folk music, and the boys and girls love it. If you plan to teach budgeting in your math class, have the youngsters work out budgets for themselves, or for a brother or sister in college. If a foreign film is seen, have them see it without titles, so they have to try to comprehend the language.

In any discussion, constantly ask, "What do you think?" Or "What would you have done?" Or "Can you see why this person acted in this way?" Be personal.

Immerse Yourself in Your Subject

Read, take courses in colleges and other places, attend lectures, travel. In this way, you learn about things of interest that are out of the ordinary, that are not found in texts or in the encyclopedias. Make being in your class an experience for your children. The curiosities, the tidbits, even the gossip which you can quote, are often the most stimulating part of a lesson. Word derivations can frequently be used to add a fillip, for example. Sad or happy incidents and personal stories are all more fascinating than mere facts. Quotations, too, are excellent. For instance, Thomas Jefferson was a widower for many years of his life, and one might feel he was lonely living in Monticello. But no, his daughter and son-in-law lived there with him, and they had many children to fill the house. Mark Twain, while a very famous writer, was almost always in financial difficulties—like some of the famous folk of today. And, of course, where did the name come from which made Samuel Clemens famous? These are the bits we mean—personal details which transform the famous man into a human being.

Competitions for Grades, for Glory, or for Both

Bees similar to the old-fashioned spelling bee, can be used in any subject area to add excitement. You may establish teams—boys versus girls, or any other division you see fit, and run a series of competitions. Stress, though, that this is a personal effort on the part of each and every child. You may wish to give credit toward the grade; the winner could receive three points added to his report card mark, the runner-up two. Have the class secretary post the results on a chart, and twice during the year award the credit. Or you may prefer to give prizes, such as books. Ask the chairman of your department for any sample copies which might be available, or write to the book publishers, on school stationery, requesting books to be used for the purpose mentioned. The school stockroom should be perused, for on its shelves you may locate items which will serve as prizes—packages of construction paper or paints, for example.

It is possible to have your own World Series of Learning. Call your teams the American and the National Leagues, consider the competitions ball games, and the final ones the World Series. Get excited yourself—you will communicate this to your children. Parents may be invited to share the events with the class. Remember, each contest must be a new one, with the entire class participating. No child should be merely an observer. As a child makes an error, he leaves the competition, but he should take part as a scorekeeper or as a cheerleader. (If you can tolerate noise permit cheering, but make strict rules beforehand so that the children know the limits of the games.)

When you prepare the questions, remember it is easier to use questions which are answered by one or two words. For example, instead of asking, "What is a noun?" you would phrase it, "The name given to a person, place, or thing is a ...."

48

This is a wonderful way to review vocabulary. Do not use terribly long, involved definitions. Use a dictionary developed for boys and girls. For example, "What word has the meaning, 'To seek to attain something?' " (*aspire*), or "Dull, having a thick or unsharpened edge?" (*blunt*). "A meeting of members of a political party to make plans for the future?" (*caucus*).

Link Your Subject to Possible Vocations

Allow your pupils to gain experiences as they research various subject areas. Language arts, for instance, leads to journalism, to all varieties of writing—plays, novels, nonfiction—and to teaching. It may also lead to acting, to broadcasting, to doing critical analysis. You may have your children select a field in which they have some interest and do an investigation of it. The future and the occupations a child chooses are of the greatest importance to him. Too often there is little or no cognizance taken of this in school. You can give an assignment such as the following:

> **Interview someone working in the occupation of your choice.** *Learn from him: 1. Does he like the work? Why? If not, why not? 2. How long did it take him to prepare for this? 3. How (what schooling did he have)? 4. What does he actually do during a day at work? 5. How does the salary he earns compare with other occupations?*

Have your children give reports to their classmates, so that the information each obtained is available to everyone. Discuss it, so that the entire group gains some awareness of the world of work.

Make Being in Your Room, Physically, an Experience in Itself

Encourage your children to bring in objects of interest that will make the room attractive. In the lower grades, items for "show and tell" might be retained in the classroom for a period of time. Doll collections, rock or leaf collections, stamps, coins, chess pieces—the variety is endless. Be sure everything brought in is kept under lock and key. Children are easily tempted to "borrow" things, meaning to return them, but this leads to a great deal of difficulty. If any objects remain in school, you, the teacher, must take the responsibility for it.

49

Figure 2-2

Begin by bringing in intriguing items yourself, and by your example the children will follow suit. Offer credit, of course, for their efforts. One youngster brought in a rather unusual object, a cross between an orange and a grapefruit, most aptly named "ugly fruit." It has the good features of neither. Many museums, such as the American Museum of Natural History in New York City, have circulating exhibits with dioramas suitable for social studies and language arts classes, as well as the scientific materials you would expect.

Do you collect souvenirs as you travel? These are wonderful "conversation pieces." Even the picture postcards you receive are good. And many of your boys and girls may have the same type of thing to offer. We proudly exhibited stones from the Roman Forum and from the top of Mount Vesuvius next to petrified wood from the souvenir shops bordering the "petrified forest." Shells from a local seashore, fossils from a favorite picnic spot, dolls representing historical characters or geographical areas—any and everything is worthwhile. The science storeroom may be raided, for many of the prepared specimens are excellent for permanent exhibits. The experience of seeing actual embryos of frogs and birds, for example, is a particularly memorable one. There are generally models of parts of the body, or of plants and animals, on its shelves. Small working machines, too, provide interest and require a minimum of effort on your part.

Artwork by your children, or their parents or relatives, is wonderful. Put your imagination to work; enlist that of your children. The world is your supply house. Happy hunting.

It is from experiences such as these that children are stimulated to grow and develop. They often do not get the proper mental stimulation from books and printed materials, but they do get it from being in an unusual, bright, imaginative place.

Fun and Games

There are a great many times when you may feel that both you and your children are a bit bored, and that you want to perk things up a bit. Perhaps you have covered all of the material you had planned, or you are teaching a class you do not ordinarily teach. Often, too, before a holiday, when it is difficult to hold your children's attention, you may want experiences which are unusual. We suggest these activities which we call "fun and games." Your children will benefit immeasurably, for you may change possible negative attitudes toward school by making it a pleasant place in which to be.

1. *Acting.* Almost all children love to act—even the most bashful of us—and charades in class are a wonderful way to utilize this love. All of the children are brought in, so to speak, and can enjoy the situation. Boys may be teamed against girls, or the students may be grouped in any way you or they prefer. Perhaps the subject you teach may be linked to the game—excellent; but, even if it cannot be, the game may be played anyway, with historical events, stories from literature, or scientific discoveries.

2. *Playlets-on-the-spot.* Other forms of acting are good, too; with a guidance purpose, you may set up groups of children, and give each

a subject on which a playlet may be devised. Parent-child relationships lend themselves to this. For example:

    a. Family scene—son caught smoking by his father.
    b. Brother caught stealing by his sister.
    c. Child brings home a poor report card.
    d. "When I am old enough to date, to work."
    e. "How to budget my spending."
    f. "How shall we dress for school?"
    g. "Old enough to fight, old enough to vote?"
    h. "My little sister (or brother) always takes my things."

You may want your students to suggest topics, or they may dramatize other personal experiences they feel would interest their classmates.

3. *Old plays in modern dress.* Let your class, divided into groups, select a theme from an old play, a historical event, a scene from the Bible, or a part of a book they have enjoyed and act out any of these scenes. No need to prepare a formal script. Set the scene and have the boys and girls fill in the dialogue.

Selection of your group is important because you must have at least one extrovert in each group to lead it. Other children will surprise you with their talents, but be sure you choose carefully. Explain to your pupils that, in order for these activities to succeed, they must literally "let themselves go,"—throw themselves into the spirit of the occasion. They must use their imaginations, lose their identities, and become the character they are portraying. With your urging they are able to do this, and enjoy themselves tremendously. Many a shy, backward child loses his inhibitions, takes part in the playlets, and displays considerable talent. The shy child is very often a sensitive child, and sensitivity is often accompanied by imaginative powers.

Decorating

Before a holiday, particularly, you will find your pupils enjoy drawing murals on the boards and doing various other types of decorating. Give them a theme, materials, and allow them to create. Many may work with construction paper; others have a wonderful time with colored chalk. The results will delight you, but the benefits are from the activity itself.

Guessing Games

1. The old favorite, "20 Questions," about persons, places, or things works well in a classroom situation. Select a child to be the mentor.

Official Photograph—Board of Education, City of N.Y

Figure 2-3

He decides on the subject, and the other students then ask questions to elicit information concerning it. If they cannot guess correctly, the mentor wins the point. If they do, the child who won the point becomes the mentor.

2. Riddles are wonderful all the time. Call them "Instant Concentration," if you prefer. Present these, and see how quickly they will stimulate the children.

"Jack and Jill are found dead on the floor. Near them is a pile of broken glass and some water. They died by suffocation. How was this possible? What happened to Jack and Jill?"

Then offer to answer all questions.

"No, they did not commit suicide,"—that's usually the first question. And they'll go on and on. Actually this is a case of "mental set"— children often do better with such a puzzle than adults because their

53

mental set is not as rigid. When we hear names, we immediately think of human beings. In this riddle Jack and Jill were goldfish.

Children Teaching the Class

Ask your children if they would like to have a chance to teach a lesson. If they seem to like the idea, they will benefit a great deal from the experience. You may wish to have them elect a child or you may assign someone. In either event, plan the lesson with the youngster; help him to prepare every bit of the work in advance and assist him in gathering the materials he needs. While he is teaching, stand by, but do not interfere unless it is absolutely necessary. Once you try this method, if you find you like it, give the opportunity to as many children as possible. You will probably find that the child's lesson will be very similar to yours in form and approach, for do we not learn a great deal by example?

Keeping a Notebook and Copying Notes

In order to learn to write, a child must write. The repetition of the physical act is necessary if he is to master this. We almost take handwriting for granted, and the resultant penmanship of many children often leaves much to be desired. Keeping a good notebook, with notes of value, affords practice in the skill of writing, and can be used to give the child a feeling of satisfaction and achievement which he desperately needs. We believe that when a child can show you a fine notebook, he feels he has really worked hard. To increase the notebook's value and build a success pattern with the child, have him gather photos and newspaper clippings. Keep these in a "Current Events" section (which is directly related to language arts or social studies), scientific current events, or a section on "Figures in the News."

Give credit for the notebook; indeed make it one part of the child's grade, and you will find your pupils will be happier as a result, for it is a task well within the range of every child's ability.

Writing on the Blackboard

Children love to write on the board. Have your boys and girls do so, frequently. This is a motivational experience and supplies physical activity. The work is easily checked and corrected, too, making your task simpler.

You may utilize this technique in every subject area, using questions of a short-answer variety. It is obvious that this method is useful for teaching mathematics or arithmetic, but it can be used most effectively in vocabulary building. Place a long word on the board (for years it was Constantinople). Divide the class into teams; boys against girls is usually fun. Ask for each child to write a word on the board as soon as he thinks of it, using the letters in the word. To make the game valuable, demand words of five letters or more. From "transportation," for example, we were given the following from a slow eighth-grade group: "rotation," "ration," "nation," "transport," "sport," "transit." After the game has been won, define each word and use it in a sentence. If you find there is insufficient activity with five-letter words, ask for words of four letters. This will increase the speed of the game.

Conclusion

Our aim in writing this chapter has been twofold. On one hand, we have sought to bring you a variety of experiences which will stimulate your children and make them work with you, rather than be mere observers of the classroom scene. We suggest you hold treasure hunts to get them into motion. Trips to the theatre or the movies may be a very valuable adjunct in your work, if used judiciously. Publishing class newspapers and magazines provides many learning experiences; debates, "overtime work," competitions are suggested. Children should be encouraged to make contributions to the class of interesting materials. Methods for injecting humor are included in a section called, "Fun and Games," and your children will find the activities attractive.

Our second aim has been to stimulate you to become creative, to use your imagination to give your children a plethora of experiences, to intrigue them, to supply them with things to talk and think about. Teaching is indeed an art, but like every other artist, we must constantly work to improve our techniques.

Alexander King, in "Is There a Life After Birth?" wrote of one of his teachers thusly:

"If you're lucky and you get the right break, then your English teacher will be in love with his subject, and the whole world of great literature will open up all of its treasures to you. If your man (or woman), on the other hand, happens to be just a job-holding timeserver, then I am afraid, the chances are pretty strong that a deadly load of wretchedly written magazine articles and a slew of idiotically contrived comic books will eventually become the basic foundation for your intellectual diet."

We can never forget that the influence we have on children is tremendous. Today, perhaps more than ever before, it is important that we give them a great many new, interesting, and stimulating learning experiences.

··· **3** ···

Self-Discipline Through Understanding the Value of Education

In order to carry on an effective experiential learning program, we believe you must first develop in your pupils attitudes of cooperation and involvement, for if your pupils are not with you, they are "agin'" you. The saying, new to the seventies, sums it up, "If you are not part of the solution, you're part of the problem." So it is with your students. If they are not participating, they are not learning. Therefore, we feel, your first task must be to create attitudes in them which make them realize the fact that their schoolwork is their labor, that it is important to them, and, if they realize this, their lives will be richer, happier, and more successful. You must attempt to make them "tune you in," and work along with you and with their classmates.

We have developed a hypothesis to explain why many children become bored, do not participate in the learning process, lose all signs of interest, and eventually fall into the category of the behavior problem. We believe it is because they do not realize that getting an education is so important to them, personally. They do not see the connection between the work they are doing now, and their future occupations. The world, for them, consists of the here and now—with never a thought for the day after tomorrow. Their physical needs—food, shelter, and clothing—are met by their parents, and the realization that they will, at some future time, have to be financially responsible, rarely, if ever, enters their minds. School is considered, by most of our children, to be "pass" time, rather than "work" time. Accordingly, they are observers, rather than participants. It is this attitude which will do them irreparable harm. If we can change this— if we can make them see that the experiences they have in school do have merit, are relative to their lives, and will help them in the future —we can change their negative approach. We can motivate them to impose self-discipline, based on the fact that they realize they have a need for education and are willing to work to fulfill it.

We shall suggest an experimental questionnaire for your children to answer. It will show you how your youngsters really feel about attending school. We will then discuss and interpret the results we have obtained with this series of questions. A specific plan follows which you may use. It strongly emphasizes the value of education. Another questionnaire is included to help you focus your children's thinking in terms of goals. There are techniques listed for instilling the concept of self-discipline with children, and you will find specific suggestions for teaching practical topics within the subject areas. Various methods of handling specific problems are suggested which emphasize a positive approach—by developing rapport with your children, by giving them status, by treating them fairly at all times. Through exemplifying good manners and respect for the individual, you bring out these qualities in your children, and you emphasize the concept of self-discipline. If you are having difficulty with an entire class, a "notebook completion week" is outlined, which will keep the boys and girls gainfully employed and help settle them down to work.

The children will realize that by behaving well they receive more from you—and that what you are giving to them is very, very valuable.

THE QUESTIONNAIRE—"WHY DO I GO TO SCHOOL?"

Administering It

To find out the answer to this very important question, we suggest you utilize the series of questions below. Rexograph the questionnaire and distribute it. Tell your children they do not have to give you this information, but it is in the nature of an experiment which will help all of you. There is no need for them to sign their names, but be sure to remind them that honesty is essential.

These are the questions:

1. How old are you?
2. For how many years have you been in school?
3. How many children are there in your family?
4. Why do you go to school?
5. In what way will school help you in your present life?
6. In what way do you think school will help your future life?
7. Which subject or subjects do you think will help you most in your future life?
8. Which subject will be of the least value?

9. Would you come to school if you didn't have to come?
10. How could school be made more meaningful for you?

Please emphasize the need for truthful answers, and promise to review them with the boys and girls, afterwards, without disclosing any identities. After they have written their replies to number 4, ask them to give another response if theirs was funny. If theirs was serious, and they would like to give a funny one, permit them to do so now.

All too often we have found children do not see any connection between their schooling and their future lives. Let us give you a sample of some of the replies we have received. Incidentally, we use the first three questions to relax the children, to get their brains and fingers working, and to take them "off their guard." Question number 4 is, of course, the first of real significance.

Results

Here are some sample answers to number 4. (Why do you go to school?)

1. My parents make me.
2. If I stay home, it's against the law and I could go to jail.
3. To see my friends and have fun.
4. I need an education to get a job.
5. Sometimes it's interesting.
6. I like the school lunches.
7. I like to learn about new things.
8. I can show my friends my clothes.

Some of the replies were trite; with anonymity promised, this is to be expected. Others find the food in school superior to what they get at home. If children have run into difficulty with the attendance laws, they are well aware of the problems which arise when they do not attend school. Surely the parents' role is important, too, in school attendance, for if they have a cavalier attitude, the students surely will. But the three comments which have the most significance for us are, of course, "I need an education," "Sometimes school is interesting," and "I like to learn about new things."

Unless we become press agents and publicize our product, unless we stress the need for education and the connection between it and an interesting, useful, and productive life, we are losing sight of its most important aspects—we are simply missing the boat.

There cannot be a teacher alive who is not convinced of the value of education. This is basic to our work, to our lives, and to our effect on our children. Not an abstract concept, this is a matter of extreme practicality—of cold cash. Make no mistake—the pupils who are your most severe discipline problems, need an education to improve their lives by improving their earning ability.

HOW CAN WE STRESS THE VALUE OF EDUCATION?

1. Discuss with your classes the concept, "Education Pays." Make sure your children are made aware of the different skills, and how much possession of them is worth in terms of weekly, monthly, or yearly salary. Encourage them to talk about their own knowledge—what they have heard from their parents, their friends, their neighbors.

2. You may wish to have a representative of the United States Employment Service come up to speak to your class. This is easily arranged by a telephone call to the local office.

3. Have at your disposal statistics to prove what you are saying. You may wish to rexograph the table below and distribute copies to the children.

   a. Work with these figures. Have the pupils translate them into terms of their own lives. How much can one earn in his lifetime if he has graduated from high school? From college? How much does this mean per week? Per month?

   b. Show how much an investment of four years of college education will yield.

(Include a graph)

INCOME FROM AGE 18 UNTIL ONE'S DEATH

Over 4 yrs.	$5 4 2, 0 0 0	College
4 yrs.	$5 0 8, 0 0 0	College
1 to 3 yrs.	$3 9 4, 0 0 0	College
4 yrs.	$3 4 1, 0 0 0	High School
1 to 3 yrs.	$2 8 4, 0 0 0	High School
8 yrs.	$2 4 7, 0 0 0	Elementary
Less than	$1 8 9, 0 0 0	Elementary

Source: Current Population Reports
August, 1968
Bureau of Census

TEACHING TOPICS, STRESSING THEIR PRACTICAL VALUE

In your work with your classes, regardless of the subject area, choose topics with practical value.

1. Units on careers may be incorporated into almost any subject area. The purpose of this unit is to have the child obtain specific information about a job in which he is interested. However, choose two jobs in the area—one skilled and the other unskilled, so that a comparison may be made. For example, in regard to hospital work, a boy might compare the orderly with the technician, the bacteriologist with the physician. A girl might compare cashiering with secretarial work, selling with buying. (Not consumer buying, but the buying done by the executives of department stores.)

To make this project as experiential as possible, have the children prepare reports which require them to interview people actually earning their livings working at the jobs. If they need your assistance in locating such persons, writing letters to big companies, stores, or organizations usually produces the necessary contacts. Discuss the reports in class, always showing the connection between education and earnings.

A report might consist of the following information obtained from one or several people employed in the job:

a. Do you like the work?
b. What do you do every day?
c. What does this job pay to people just starting in it?
d. How much can you go up to?
e. How did you get the job?
f. What education did you need for it?
g. Are there chances for advancement?
h. Would you recommend the work to a young person? To me?

As you can see, this is a very practical list. It would give a child a good deal of information, which he may then discuss with his parents. After that, he would write up his report and be ready to discuss it in class.

2. In mathematics, you have a wonderful opportunity to "sneak" these concepts in very frequently. In solving problems, your children can calculate earnings and see benefits themselves. A problem might read, "A boy who takes a job in a grocery store earns $1.75 per hour. His friend can type, so she is able to find work paying $2.50 per hour. How much is the ability to type worth in terms of a 40-hour week?"

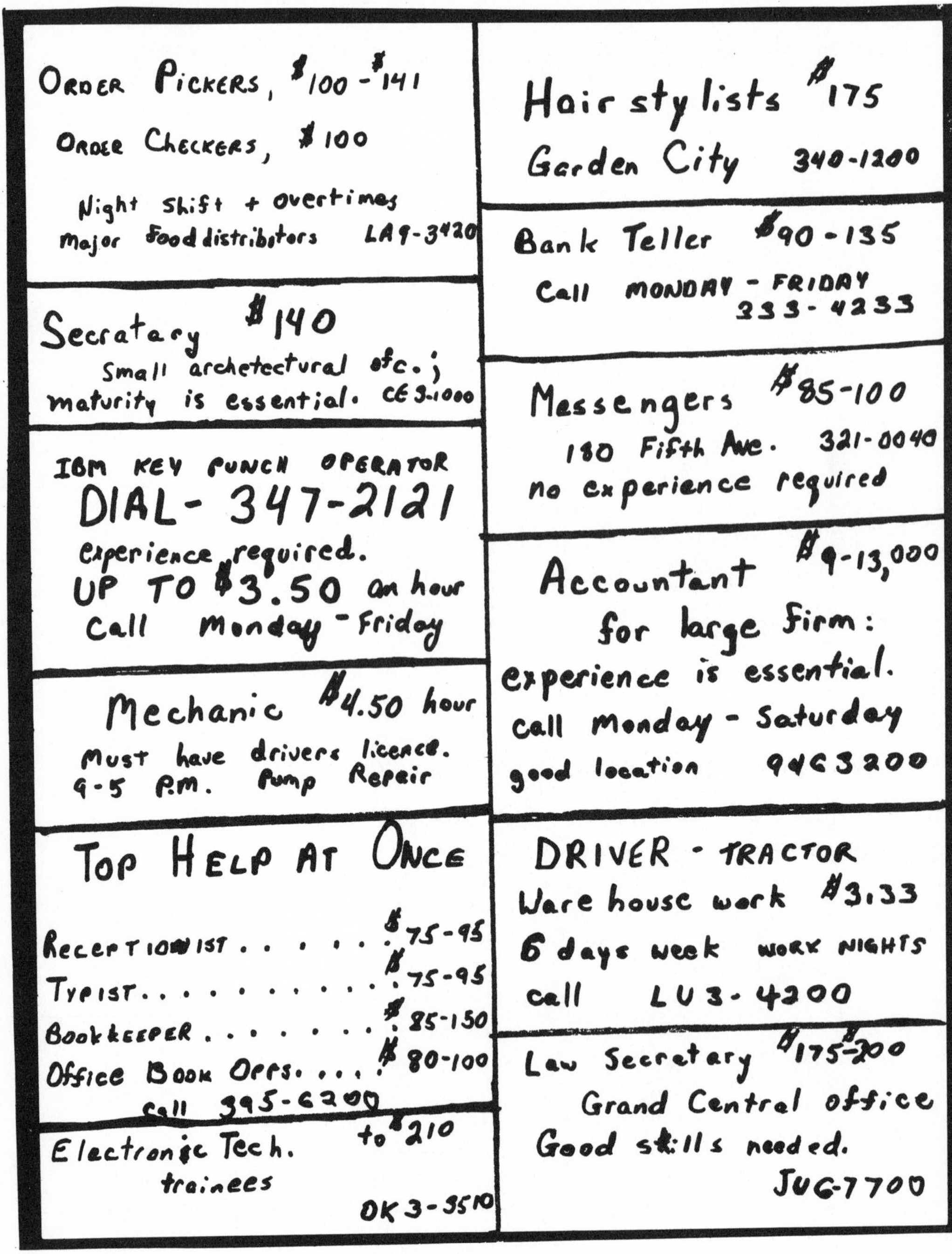

ORDER PICKERS, $100-$141

ORDER CHECKERS, $100

Night shift + overtimes
major food distributors   LA9-3420

Secretary $140
    Small archetectural ofc.;
maturity is essential. CE3-1000

IBM KEY PUNCH OPERATOR
DIAL- 347-2121
experience required.
UP TO $3.50 an hour
Call   Monday - Friday

Mechanic $4.50 hour
Must have drivers licence.
9-5 P.M.   Pump Repair

TOP HELP AT ONCE

RECEPTIONIST $75-95
TYPIST $75-95
BOOKKEEPER $85-150
Office Book Offs. $80-100
        call 395-6200

Electronic Tech.   to $210
    trainees
                OK3-9510

Hair stylists $175
Garden City   340-1200

Bank Teller $90-135
    Call   MONDAY - FRIDAY
                333-4233

Messengers $85-100
    180 Fifth Ave.   321-0040
no experience required

Accountant $9-13,000
    for large firm:
experience is essential.
call Monday - Saturday
good location   9463200

DRIVER - TRACTOR
Ware house work $3.33
6 days week   WORK NIGHTS
call   LU3-4200

Law Secretary $175-200
    Grand Central office
Good skills needed.
                JU6-7700

Figure 3-1

64

If you train yourself to think in this manner, you will find many places to inject the philosophy. In studying graphs, for example, or in calculating percentages, how simple it is to bring in the unskilled workers' salary versus the skilled.

3. In language arts, use "want ads" for one unit. Give the children experiences reading them, deciding which jobs interest them, writing letters for interviews. Prepare rexographed applications for the children to fill in—to give them experience in this very important skill. You can obtain actual applications from the United States Civil Service Commission, and from local and state systems, as well. This unit of work should be repeated year after year—so that the students become so familiar with the forms that they are not intimidated by them.

Be sure to call to the children's attention the fact that this reading and writing is essential in finding a job.

Have the children choose advertisements that interest them, and write them on charts. Follow this with discussion.

HANDLING PROBLEMS

1. If a class or a student or two misbehaves, and you must use disciplinary measures, we suggest you use the approach, "You are cheating yourself, and your classmates, by making it impossible for me to teach. I will be paid the same salary whether I teach you or act as a policeman. But you need what I can teach you. You need to get an education. Now it's up to you. Do I teach, or police?" If it is one or two children who are disruptive, talk to them privately, stressing this approach—providing you truly believe it. We have often used the metaphor, "We pitch, but you must be there to catch—or there is no ball game. I don't need the game, but you do!"

We must understand and appreciate the child's position. It may be difficult for him to comprehend why he must come to school. In some classes he may not have any idea of what is going on, and in others he couldn't care less. We repeat many times, and we know you'll agree it bears repetition—the children must have experience in practical skills, so that they see the relationship between what they are learning and how they will be able to use it in the future.

2. *"Why Didn't You Tell Us?"*: If you wish to develop closeness with your children, you may wish to tell them this story. You may say it happened to a friend of yours, because it is true, and it did happen to me. Several years ago, on my way home by public transportation, I met a young fellow who recognized me, called me by name, and came over to talk to me. We carried on an animated conversation, though I really didn't remember him—although he did look familiar.

He told me he had a job, but it didn't pay very much, and he wanted to get married, but realized his income was inadequate. After some time, he said to me, "You really don't remember exactly who I am, do you?" I had to admit, rather shamefacedly, that I was afraid I didn't. He watched my expression as he said, "I was in class ———. I'm John Doe." Inadvertently I gasped, and actually murmured, "I don't believe it." Normally, I would never have responded this way, but it seemed impossible that a child who had been so disturbed, and disturbing, could have matured into this serious, mannerly young man. John had been one of the children in the first class I taught, and had given me many, many sleepless nights, trying to think of ways to teach and control him.

We continued our conversation. John said something which I have never forgotten, and which really had a profound effect on my professional life subsequently.

"Why didn't you tell us?" he asked.

"Tell you what?"

"What a difference it makes if you finish school! How much more money you can get! What kind of a job can I find now? How can I get married on my income? Why didn't you tell us?"

And, indeed, it is our job to tell them—over and over again, that they cannot waste this time—that these years in school are very precious, and that they are deciding now whether they will succeed or fail. We say, now, to our children, "What you do for the first 20 years of your life will affect you for the next 50, 60, or 70. Even the pension one gets is determined by the work he did."

3. *Opportunity Knocks*: Let us impress upon the children that they have many opportunities for self-improvement and for achieving desirable goals in life by traveling along the broad highways of education. No, the streets are not paved with gold, but nevertheless, now, more than ever before, the opportunities are available. President Johnson had stated, "No child is to be deprived of an education for lack of funds." This is true for every child in our nation, Negro and white, Puerto Rican and Indian, Chinese or Japanese. It is up to us, the teachers, to be sure they understand this. We suggest you point out, also, that education is the key, too, for the person who does not plan to or want to go to college. He must learn skills which he will be able to offer to an employer. They may be in the commercial area or the vocational; they may be in retailing or in art, in hair dressing or auto mechanics, in computer operation or electronics. Far too often our children do not become aware of this need for skills (and the possibility of learning them without attending college). We are in a position to impress this upon them. Dr. Joseph Loretan, Deputy

Superintendent of the New York City School System, many years ago encouraged teachers to help boys and girls find their talents, their interests. This advice becomes more important as our century grows older, and we become more and more of a technological society. Is it not possible that the time will come when no one will be employable if he is unskilled? But how will our youngsters know this if they never learn it from us? Even the fifth-grade child can understand this concept and start looking around at the jobs in the community. And if he is made aware of the connection between this and his schoolwork, he will start disciplining himself!

Another device to impress our students with the need for skills, and initiate their thinking in this area, is by use of another questionnaire. Encourage honesty and, since this is for the child's use, you may keep it anonymous if you wish.

4. *Your Future:*

a. In what field would you like to work when you complete your schooling?

b. Will you be prepared to enter this field?

c. Would you be willing to prepare for this job?

d. Are you preparing for it now? How?

e. What is the salary paid for this type of work?

These responses, too, should be discussed and pursued. You will probably find enough material for many hours of classwork. Each occupation may be covered—in terms of preparation, salary, etc. The children may be given assignments such as those outlined for career units. But it is important that they see a connection between their future work and their schoolwork. For example, if they are aware that a pattern of lateness today may mean trouble tomorrow, they may become punctual. There are a great many ways to tie in their lives in the world of work with school, and the more times you are able to connect the two, the better.

5. *Setting Up Goals:* With those pupils who are discipline problems, we suggest you speak to them, privately. Search out their goals, their ambitions. You'll often find there aren't any. This is where you may have a profound effect on the child. Try to help him find an area which will serve as a goal—even a temporary one. It is surprising how many boys will react favorably if you suggest becoming a policeman or a fireman. These are, to children, prestigious jobs. Stress, "This goal is temporary; you may change it any time!" We have seen this technique have a very salutary effect. Afterwards say, "Now we must help you work toward it." It is then up to you to do so. You may assign a report—have the child interview people actually engaged in the occupation. We suggest it would be advisable to have

them report their findings to the class, being sure to include the requirements for the job, so that the need for training and education is evident.

You may decide to discuss some of the occupations for girls which necessitate schooling—but not college. Nursing, beauty culture, and secretarial work are but a few. In a class discussion, you may wish to use these as starters and then elicit further information from your children.

Consider the fact that many of your youngsters may be growing up in homes where education is not held in high esteem. Indeed, it is surprisingly often decried. While it is true some parents regret the fact that they were unable, for one reason or another, to graduate from high school, or even from elementary school, far too often this feeling is concealed. It takes a secure person to say, "I made a mistake. I should have stayed in school."

In many homes there is no father, and no one to exemplify and extol the benefits of education. What is sadder for a young person to see, than a parent going from one unskilled job to another? Yet children are unable to think of themselves in such situations. They have difficulty projecting themselves ahead. However we have found one way to do this. We ask the pupils if they remember the day John F. Kennedy was assassinated. Then we ask, "What specifically do you remember?" After a short discussion, we make the point—that was "X" years ago. In what grade were you? (Let them figure this out.) Then say, "Doesn't that seem like yesterday? Well, 'X' years from today you will be graduating from high school" (or whatever grade they will be in)—and so emphasize the fleeting of time and how precious and few the school years are. You may wish to show them they are almost defenseless without an education, and ask, "What are you doing with your time? What training are you preparing for? Will you be able to do something which will enable you to earn a living?"

Very often even the most hardened child will react, and may even become interested in school. Your sincerity, your enthusiasm, and your conviction will be contagious. You must show him education really does pay.

6. *You May Wish to Use This Procedure:*

    a. Questionnaire—Why Do I Go to School?

    b. Discussion of results of questionnaire.

    c. Discussion of graph on page 62.

    d. Questionnaire—Your Future.

    e. Discussion of replies.

    f. Assign reports—individual or committee, in regard to jobs mentioned in Item 4.

    g. Have children give reports—discuss with entire class after each report is given.

7. *Never Feel You Must Lie to Children:* The truth is far more effective. For example, you should be able to say truthfully to a child, "You are an intelligent person. I cannot understand why you are disrupting your class, unless it is perhaps because you don't realize how important your job in school is. We're training you to earn a living. You do plan to work someday, don't you?"

Children love "heart-to-heart" talks. As they approach the age of puberty they have conflicts and questions. All too often they have no opportunity to ask about these, and your interest will do much to help them. The disturbing child is often an attention-seeker, and, if you give him an opportunity to get this attention in an acceptable manner, you can help eliminate some, if not all, of the disruptiveness.

In a heart-to-heart talk, sometimes you need say little or nothing. Try to allow the child to talk. If he doesn't, then you should, of course, try to draw him out with questions. You will sometimes find an amazing improvement in your relationship as a result of having tried to talk to him.

8. *Another Way to Improve Your Discipline Is to Ask for the Children's Cooperation:* Far too often this obvious procedure is forgotten. It is, however, always worth trying. The "we" approach, "What can we do to improve learning in this class?", is good. Get ideas from the children. You will be surprised to learn how practical some are. Ask, "How many of you think you can cooperate?" If one or two children say no, speak to them privately. They may want attention or they may have real problems.

Every teacher of children has some problems. Do not be discouraged when your discipline doesn't reach every child. We are all perfectionists, but we have to learn that "you can't win them all." Nor can you expect to. But we have found, with most normal, healthy children, you can win very often.

9. *Never Lose Your Sense of Fairness:* Perhaps the aspect of behavior which most upsets children (and adults) is favoritism. If you have your "pets," you create a bad climate in your classroom. You cause resentments to build up, a lack of respect for you develops, and quarrels and fights erupt. It's such a human failing to respond favorably to the sweet, cooperative child—who's usually bright, pleasant, and only too willing to work like a slave for you. Do not let this situation arise. Try to treat every child in the same way. Each child needs your approval and affection.

69

Giving a "troublemaker" status by making him a monitor will help improve your discipline, providing he knows it is *not* a bribe. Never permit a child to think he intimidates you, or that you are buying him. If you can make him believe you think he is a worthwhile human being, and give him tasks he can do, you may be able to rehabilitate even the most difficult. Many of these children are rarely spoken to with kindness or with any sort of understanding. They almost never are able to achieve well, and they need your help and compassion. Say, "You know you can be a big help to me rather than a hindrance, because you are an intelligent person."

10. *"Notebook Completion Week":* Many young people are hyperactive. They seem to have too much energy. If you do not keep them busy and happy, they become disruptive. If you are having discipline problems, start a "notebook completion week" or month. Give many notes, lots of writing. Have the pupils work from almost the minute they enter until the time they leave. To relieve the tedium, omit key words, and, as they are copying the notes, the students fill in the blank spaces.

This is useful in any subject, and will settle the most difficult classes. You may stress the need to complete the notebook in this manner:

"We have to be sure you have a complete set of all of the notes you will need to review. To help you review, right now we are leaving blanks for you to fill in, then we will go over them." For example, The parts of speech, which show action or state of being are ....
An example of an action verb is .... An example of a state of being verb is .... We may show emotion with verbs. For example, one showing happiness is .... To show sadness, we may say we .... To show surprise, I ...., and I might .... when I'm frightened.

Your notes should, however, be of value. Then be sure they are copied correctly and use the material covered to write your examinations. In this way your pupils will feel the notetaking is worthwhile, worth their time and energy.

11. If you are having difficulty with your classes, review your previous behavior with them. There is the possibility you will not be able to completely eliminate the problems, but by analyzing them you will be able to avoid them next year. Some problems may, however, be solved. First, begin by giving written work. If anyone refuses to do it, show him why he should—what value it will have for him in the future. Don't get angry or upset, but speak calmly and as dispassionately as possible. Regard this as one of your greatest chal-

lenges—to convert a child from hostility to cooperation. The conversation might go:

"Bill, why don't you do your work?"

"I don't like to do it."

"Can you? If you can't, let me help you with it."

"I can."

"Fine. You know I think you're an intelligent boy. If you haven't been shown how to interpret a paragraph, let's do it now."

"No."

"Well, Bill, I want you to know I want to help you. Let's see just how well the whole class can handle it."

Bill is reluctant, he's ashamed, and he has to cover up his own inadequacies. But, by showing kindness and consideration, you will eventually reach him. Remember, it can't be done by threats or by screaming. Instead make Bill, and the others like him, want to please you.

12. If you are every inch the lady or gentleman, and you expect your children to behave in the same way, your discipline will be based on mutual respect and admiration. This is absolutely the best kind. Not only are you well treated, but also you raise the children to your level. Do not mistake manners for lack of firmness. Far from it, the person who never has to raise his or her voice must have far more intestinal fortitude. But he conveys his strength of character; it is apparent to the children. A soft voice, a nice smile, a firm hand, and the distinct feeling "I am the teacher; I'm here to teach you" or "I'm surprised at you, Jack. I know you're interested in your work," may accomplish wonders for you.

We have outlined a number of ways in which you can improve your discipline. None of these is punitive. All are based on the concept "Every child is educable, needs his education, and is in school to get it." It is a question of reaching him through the proper channels. It is our job to help him prepare for his place in the world of work—a special place based on his own particular skills. We must help him see that he needs what we are able to teach him, and that it is not fair to allow him or any other pupil to prevent the class from getting it. We seek to discover his talents and abilities and to help develop them, never failing to try to foster the development of his self-esteem as well. This behavior will preclude exhibitions or disruptions on his part. You are his teacher—therefore, his friend. If you really are, he will feel it and appreciate it. Of course you will always

Dear Mrs. Karlin,

My class and I would like to thank you for the advise that you gave to our class 7-347. We really and truly appreciate what the teachers do for us. You gave us very good advise yesterday. I give you my word that 7-347 and myself will try very hard so that we can get a good job. I hope that no one else will not drop out of school. Some children today just don't seem to realize that to get a good job you need a good education; to get a better job you need to have a good education (High school deplomer) and a college deplomer. We want to show the teachers that we are grown up enough and we want to show them that we can work and be good if we want. a teacher can teach for 8 hours but if we are not paying attention we wont learn anything. You said that thats just like throwing a ball at someone but if they dont catch it what's the sense of throwing it. We are going to catch that ball. We will try our best.

Very sincerly,

7-347

Figure 3-2

72

avoid downgrading any child, for this accomplishes less than nothing.

One of the thrills of the teaching profession is to learn that your children have taken you and your words to heart.

Recently I had occasion to speak to a rather disruptive group of youngsters. I used the approach outlined in this chapter. Two days later their art teacher asked me, "What did you do to 7-347? They're different children!" At the end of the week, I received a letter (see Figure 3–2).

Conclusion

We believe that very often children are disruptive because they are unaware of the need for, and value of, an education. We feel that all too often, insufficient time is spent on this very important concept, and that as a result many children do not participate in the learning process, and consequently —out of boredom—misbehave. We have outlined methods for bringing out to them the importance of learning, including questionnaires and discussion material. Statistics are included showing the variation in income which may be anticipated, depending on the amount of education a person receives. Information to be included in career units is suggested. Our motivation is to make the children see that they must get an education and therefore develop self-discipline.

In the previous sections, we considered the handling of problems, with an entire class or with specific children. We gave various approaches; such as, discussions in regard to "cheating oneself" and the others in the class, developing rapport through heart-to-heart talks. We suggested you work on setting up educational and vocational goals, and procedures to follow are listed if you wish to include this work as a unit. (We believe that this topic is germane and of great value to any subject—at any time in the curriculum— particularly, but not only, if you are having difficulty teaching the class.)

Requesting class cooperation, never losing your sense of fairness, giving a troublemaker status (but not bribing him) are discussed as ways of obtaining wholesome discipline. A "notebook completion week" may be the way in which you can "settle down" a group of energetic or disruptive children. We suggest a method you may wish to try to convert children's hostility to a desire to cooperate. By behaving in a manner which respects children as individuals, we believe you will find they will reciprocate.

We hope you will try to apply this philosophy because it encourages the growth of your children and because it will be so meaningful in their future lives. When they ask, "Why didn't you tell us?" we can truthfully answer, "We did—or we tried to!"

• • • 4 • • •

Experiences in Democracy; the Democratically Functioning Classroom

~~~~~~~~~~~~~~~~~~~~~~~~

"Actions speak............ ...." Most people who see this incomplete sentence automatically fill in the correct words. Don't you? This adage is especially valid in teaching, and particularly so when we teach democratic living and democratic ideals. Words are not strong enough to replace experiences. Nor can they possibly. Today, one of our most important tasks, as teachers, is to set up activities so that the children actually participate in the democratic processes. Boys and girls must have such concrete experiences because they often have difficulty in grasping abstract ideas. Routine class discussion of these subjects is totally inadequate. Lecturing may be effective at times in conveying superficial information, but it is not effective for the mastering of concepts, for real learning which extends below the surface, or for actually affecting the life of the child.

In the same way that one cannot learn to operate a car without driving it, make a souffle without beating it, master sports such as tennis or golf by merely reading an instruction manual, or draw up plans for a building without putting in doors, windows, or staircases, one cannot learn the true meaning of democracy without having opportunities to experience it. We must repeatedly furnish our children with these opportunities in our classrooms. We have stressed the need for you, the teacher, to be in control of your class at all times, and we are not altering this in any way—but our children should and must be taught self-government, as one of the most important aspects of their education. You will find a number of techniques which will foster the teaching of this self-government and cooperative living through activities in the classroom. However, these activities in no way cause you to cease being the figure of authority in the classroom. Strategies for holding the class elections, outlining the duties of officials, setting up a code of behavior, and establishing a list of disciplinary actions which may be handled by the children are suggested.

DEMOCRATIC LIVING

Class Elections

"JAMES CARSON, CLASS PRESIDENT" sounds great! Duly elected by his peers, James is impressed. But if James merely holds the title without being assigned anything specific to do, it is a sham and a waste. Let us pursue what James may do and how you may teach functioning democracy to your class. We would suggest the following:

1. Set class elections for twice each year—possibly the end of September, and of February.

2. In carrying on elections:

a. Have the entire class nominate children for the various offices. You may keep a modicum of control by not establishing beforehand how many candidates may be placed in nomination. If you find the candidates being put up are not the best possible, you are able to keep the nominations open until other children are suggested. We would say six is about the largest number desirable, although you are free to decide otherwise.

Suggest girls be elected to two offices, and boys to the other two. It is poor policy to have officers of only one sex, and even worse if they are all girls.

b. Ask any child who is nominated to leave the room while the voting is going on. This eliminates some of the hard feelings which might arise as a result of the elections.

c. Elections may be held in any grade—do not hesitate to initiate this in the first grade when children's pliant minds are very receptive to new ideas. You will find the children very enthusiastic as they go about campaigning for their candidate, and actually voting. Remember, children love to imitate adult behavior and feel that they are acting grown up.

d. Begin with the election of treasurer, then secretary, then vice-president, and finally president. This procedure, too, will help you get a better group of officers. It will require the children to think ahead and select their candidates more carefully, because the most important position is the last to be decided upon.

Official Photograph—Board of Education, City of N.Y

Figure 4-1

e. You may discover that the children have elected officers of whom you do not approve; whom you would have never selected. Nevertheless, work with these children, and you will find that in many cases they will grow to fit the task. In some instances we have had boys we considered to be bullies voted into positions of authority, and have seen them do amazingly well. Your guidance will make the difference between the success or failure of the democratic process in your classroom. Stress the responsibilities the offices carry with them. Say to the class officers, "You have been elected one of our class officers. This is a very great honor, and I know you will do everything in your power to live up to it. You have certain responsibilities to yourself and to your classmates. I know you will carry them out to the very best of your ability."

f. Immediately have the names of the officers, written by the secretary, placed in a corner of the blackboard. Retain these at all times.

g. Give the class officers recognition and make sure they enjoy the status in the class which they should have. This will be accorded to them only if your children see by your actions that all officers are to be trusted, that the president can take over when a teacher is absent, that the vice-president is able to preside over the class "Senate," that the secretary and treasurer are given work to do and actually do it. By your manner you set the tone, and it must be one of respect. The officers and the class will respond in like manner.

We remember an occasion when the mother of the president of an elementary school's general organization entered the building. The monitors moved other parents out of the way, "The president's mother, the president's mother" they kept proclaiming. This was, indeed, a reflection of the feeling toward this boy—which also came from the principal and the entire faculty.

3. When class elections are over, carefully delineate the duties of each class officer; if possible elicit these from the children, by asking them what tasks they feel the president and the other elected officials should do. The following framework may be of help to you:

a. The president presides over the class if there is no teacher present or at any time a teacher requests him to do so. He is required to maintain order and subsequently must report to the teacher any children who do not cooperate. He must be fair and treat everyone in the class with respect. Stress the importance of electing a child with a strong personality, one the children have confidence in and who can lead them.

b. The vice-president will take over the duties of the president, if he is absent, or if he is otherwise occupied. He will also be responsible for notifying the office immediately if the teacher is absent, or if the class is in difficulty. He must be of assistance to the class president when the latter requests help.

c. The class secretary takes notes of all class meetings, takes the attendance in each class, and keeps a record of it. She also writes to or telephones absent pupils, sending them homework assignments when necessary.

d. The treasurer is in charge of collecting money whenever this task must be done; for lunches, milk, charity, or for trips. He must give each child a receipt when the amount of money he collects is large enough to warrant it.

4. We have seen varying types of children elected to class office, surprisingly function very well, and we have been aware of the beneficial effect this has had on personality development. The democratic processes suggested for your classroom will prove valuable for every

child in your class, and, incidentally, for you as well. Your class officers can remove many tedious tasks from your shoulders. Guide them well and you will be delighted with the results.

The Legislative Branch of the Class Government

1. Establish with the children a committee of the whole to function in both legislative and judicial capacities. Explain fully what these functions are. Point out that, as the Vice-President of the United States presides over the Senate, in our national government, the class vice-president will preside when the class convenes to set up laws.

2. At the first meeting of the legislature, have a series of laws drawn up to serve as a code of behavior. Encourage every child to participate in this meeting. The reason for this is of significance. In any venture, psychologists have found that if people are involved in establishing restrictions, they are far more prone to observe them.

3. Have the class secretary write these rules, or type them, on a rexograph master, and have them duplicated and distributed to the entire class. The children are to keep them in their notebooks in a section called "Our Democratic Classroom." Title these "Rules We Have Decided to Institute." The rules should be in keeping with school procedures, but be more inclusive. For example, in the event of a fire drill, every child must get on line silently and quickly. The class president leads the group; the other officers go to the end of the line. The rule is *absolute silence* throughout the drill, and all children must walk quickly, without running. Should the president be absent, the vice-president goes to the head of the line. If both president and vice-president are absent, the secretary will be the leader. A rule such as this, relatively simple, but important, can make the teacher's work far easier. The children have rules to follow and are trained in these procedures. The class officers help in the enforcement of all of the rules. Have the children suggest rules in regard to:

    a. Electing class officers.

    b. Behavior in class.

    c. While in large groups—in the schoolyard, in the assembly, or in the school cafeteria.

    d. Situations when one child copies from another.

    e. Doing homework.

    f. Settling disputes between themselves.

    g. Taking one another's property.

    h. Keeping the classroom clean.

4. If you feel the class is mature enough to mete out discipline, decisions should be made, in advance, so that no penalty will be too severe. For example, if a child consistently litters, might he not be required to pick up the papers from the floor of the entire room for several days? Other offenses which might be established as misdemeanors are:

    a. Calling out in class.
    b. Arriving late—without an acceptable excuse.
    c. Improper dress—repeatedly, after having been warned.
    d. Fighting in class, or anywhere in school.
    e. Behaving disrespectfully toward another member of the class.
    f. Behaving disrespectfully toward a teacher or another adult.
    g. Cheating or copying on an examination.
    h. Stealing.
    i. Destroying books or other property belonging to the school.
    j. Destroying property belonging to another child.

In establishing the punishments, be sure they are not too severe. They must be feasible: it is far better if they can be carried out by other children in the class, rather than by the teacher or other adults. It goes without saying that any kind of corporal punishment must always be avoided. Have the secretary write these decisions on the board, and have them copied into the children's notebooks, under the heading "Regulations in Regard to Misbehavior."

The Judicial Branch of the Class Government

When a child misbehaves, if the misdemeanor is severe, you may permit the class to hold a mock trial during which the child is tried by his peers. Allow the child to select another youngster to defend him, and the rest of the class to select a judge and a jury. Guide them in preparing their cases, in getting witnesses, and in the actual trial situation. This might prove to be an interesting experience for the children, but please be sure everyone is fairly treated and that no hard feelings result. Your careful guidance is absolutely essential.

Self-Government

1. During class trips, the class should elect sergeants-at-arms to keep the children in small groups. Divide the class into these groupings, and place one of the sergeants in charge of each. He is then made

responsible for "head counts" and for the attendance of the whole group.

2. When there are decisions to be made, which can be entrusted to the children, allow them to make them. For example, if you are asked to raise funds for a school project or for a charity, have the class make suggestions and vote on them. This method works out very well; children are imaginative, and they will suggest methods which are original and on their level.

3. Elect a committee, headed by the secretary, to telephone absentee children—to give them their homework and review the work covered that day in class. Stress the need for responsible children—give those nominated the chance to decline if they will not be able to handle the task, or if they confess to a lack of time to complete the task.

4. You will think of many other ways to teach this system of democratic functioning. Much will depend on the children in your class—on their maturity and desire to participate. You will find, though, that even the most difficult, the most hostile child will react to your fairness and positive feelings toward him and his classmates. You will build morale within the class because each child can be made to feel important—that his voice actually counts. For it does!

Through these activities, you have a chance to develop within the children an understanding of the rights and responsibilities, as well as the privileges, of a democracy. This is not something which comes easily. It will require work on your part and on the parts of the children, but they will realize that power is coupled with responsibility. They cannot make their decisions lightly; nor should they be permitted to do so.

5. Leadership qualities will emerge in the children if you permit them to actually lead. By electing officers twice a year, and by stating at the beginning of the year that no child will be permitted to serve twice, you double the opportunity for different children to gain the experience of being a class officer.

Class elections should be preceded by campaign speeches, for these give the children valid reasons to speak and build excitement into the election process. Posters, buttons, and other devices may be encouraged as well.

6. It is valuable occasionally to hold a "town hall meeting" to clear the air—this allows children to discuss their grievances. Sometimes, for example, one child "sets the class off," initiates uncooperative or disruptive behavior. You may find that, by discussion in an open forum, this sort of behavior can be curtailed. However, do not permit the children to show excessive hostility, which actually serves no purpose.

Always insist on constructive suggestions from your children. Do not settle for mere criticism. Make this plain early in the year, and you will see that the children will learn to appreciate democracy. If you insist upon constructive comments, you will often be pleasantly surprised by your children's practical suggestions.

In an atmosphere such as this, each child is encouraged to participate —because airing one's thoughts does not require any special ability, and indeed, fosters self-expression. The child who has been reluctant to speak learns that he, too, can be heard, and, if you are skillful, you will be able to encourage him to offer his opinions. As he speaks, his self-esteem is built up, his self-image improves, and his power of speech develops.

It is tremendously important for children to assume the responsibility for their actions. If treatment is fair, if the judgment is unbiased, if help is forthcoming when needed, they will not be afraid to do so. It has been our experience that most children will try very hard not to "let you down." Even more so, they do not want to disappoint their peers. For example, a child in one of our classes once telephoned one of the authors at home one afternoon. He had taken another youngster's coat home by mistake, and he had wanted to save the other child from difficulty. He asked for the child's address and took the coat to him.

Projects

1. Projects for the class to work on bring out the best in many children. One group of high school youngsters adopted the new African nation of Upper Volta and raised funds for its development. Another group, with which we were associated, collected money, working very hard to supply some of the things needed by Dr. Tom Dooley for his first hospital. At Halloween time, collecting for the United Nations Children's Fund (UNICEF) is fun, and helps other children all over the world. A project of this nature develops feelings of responsibility for one's fellowman, even in very young children.

2. The pupils in one junior high school helped several families who had lost all of their possessions in a tenement fire, by collecting food, clothing, and money. The heroine of the fire was in the eighth grade, and her classmates wanted to do something more than the rest of the classes; in a cake sale of their own, unsupervised by any adult, they sold more than $22 worth of their home-baked cakes.

It is interesting to digress for a moment. The young girl mentioned

Somerset Hills, N.J., "Exponent" Photo

Figure 4-2. Little goodwill ambassadors on humanitarian mission for world's needy children (United Nations Children's Fund).

made headlines in the local paper. She woke up in the middle of the night, smelled smoke, saw the fire, jumped out of the building, and pulled the fire alarm. She then *returned to the building, went inside,* and *awakened her family and neighbors.* Because of her heroism, no one was seriously injured. This child had a pattern of being disruptive in school. She had been referred to the dean of discipline a countless number of times. But, like Sidney Carton in *A Tale of Two Cities,* how well she had awakened to her moral responsibilities. And it is noteworthy to add that after the tragedy of the fire, and her heroic deeds, and all of the commendations that were piled high upon her head—including a special assembly program in her honor—our heroine

Leeward, Hawaii, Press Photo

Figure 4-3. Young Hawaiians join millions of other American boys and girls in devoting Halloween fun to saving children's lives (United Nations Children's Fund).

returned to her familiar pattern; she is still being referred to the dean of discipline for misbehavior.

3. Allow the students to organize their own coaching activities. Oftentimes, friendships are born of these endeavors. Here we are bolstering the very basic humanitarian concept that the strong should help the weak. In this situation one child helps another; yet both benefit thereby. We have found a child who might be weak in reading, but who does well in drawing; conversely, a child who draws well may not be particularly talented with words. Consequently, in setting up our coaching courses, might these two children not be a great help to each other? It is also noteworthy that by mutually assisting one another, the self-image of both children is nourished. In every subject area, by all means, encourage the proficient students to help those pupils who are less gifted. Incidentally, the teacher who can help each child to find his gifts is doing a great deal to foster the development and happiness of the child.

It is possible that the slow learner has no specific talent to offer in exchange. If you have guided the children, he will be able to accept help from his classmate, because he has been made to realize that at some future date he may be able to return the favor. Be sure no child doing the coaching is patronizing or overbearing, and that some rapport develops between these two children. You might influence the children by saying, "When I was in school I had trouble with spelling. One term a boy in the class helped me, and the very next year I was able to help someone else."

Freedom to Express Ideas

In all of our classes, there should be a climate set up which permits the free expression and exchange of ideas, for this is the very core of our democracy. If we are to encourage intellectual growth, we must permit the children to express their misgivings, give voice to their complaints, and in the free air of discussion, find themselves able and willing to communicate with each other and with their teacher. Is this not the very essence of free speech? But be sure that no one is ever permitted to ridicule an idea which a child may express. It may be challenged, it may be criticized, it may be disagreed with, but never, never ridiculed. Permitting freedom of expression has a wondrous effect upon children. They will find it exhilarating, and will emerge from your class refreshed rather than tired, stimulated rather than bored. It goes without saying that cruel statements, detrimental to anyone's welfare, must be firmly discouraged.

How does one go about starting discussions? You can't say, "This is discussion time." But you might say, "We have been asked by the principal for our opinions in regard to the wearing of ties. What do you think? Gentlemen, should you have to wear them?" Or, "Should we sell candy in the school cafeteria?" Or "Many young people are shooting off firecrackers. As you can imagine, this is dangerous. What can we do to stop it?" The school administration is faced, very often, with problems which actually should be decided by the children, because, as we have mentioned, when people are involved in establishing laws, they are more likely to abide by them. When children's opinions are considered, they gain tremendously in self-esteem. Of late, have not older youths, in colleges, been demanding this?

The teacher should never be an autocrat. So often the seed of intellectuality is destroyed by the person who cannot permit freedom of expression in his class because he feels that his ideas are threatened. In connection with this concept, John Stuart Mills' *Freedom of Thought and Its Expression* written many years ago, is worthy of any teacher's perusal. You will find your classes will be far more exciting for you, if you can develop enough security in yourself and your knowledge and ability, to permit this academic freedom to flourish.

Conclusion

When the children are permitted to actually participate in the building of a democracy within the classroom, hostile emotions and activities are precluded. We have suggested class elections, setting up a code of behavior, establishing disciplinary actions implemented by the children themselves, and holding trials to experientially teach the meaning of democracy and its fulfillment.

··· **5** ···

Learning from Experiences in Reading and Language Arts

〰〰〰〰〰〰〰〰〰〰〰

The transmission of one's thoughts and ideas through the spoken and written word, and the comprehension of those of another person, are the prime purposes of language. It is to this area that we must give our greatest attention—for without the abilities to do this—to speak and to write, to listen and to read—our children are tremendously handicapped. The frustration which can accompany the inability to communicate was very vividly portrayed in the play, *The Miracle Worker*, a chronicle of the early years of Miss Helen Keller, who as a baby became deaf, dumb, and blind, and who was then taught to speak by the "miracle worker," her teacher, Anne Sullivan Macy. Our children, fortunately, are, for the most part, physically able to communicate. It is our task to teach them specifically how.

Every one of the language arts skills should be taught experientially. None should be taken for granted. Listening, for example, cannot be ignored; nor can speaking. In our anxiety to teach reading and writing, we must not overlook the others—because, in addition to reading, a child must listen, and while he must write, he absolutely must be able to make himself understood through speech.

We will consider these four areas separately, giving techniques for specific experiences in each.

SPEAKING AND LISTENING

Teaching Your Children to Speak

In many homes children are not taught to speak, and there is a minimum of communication between parents, between parents and children, and even between the siblings themselves. In school, we find these children say, "Can I have this?" and point. They may not know it is called a pencil. (This is no exaggeration, for simple nouns are often unknown to them.)

This gap, then, must be filled by encouraging our boys and girls to speak by teaching them words, and by giving the children experiences in hearing good speech. To accomplish the former, we suggest that you instruct the children to answer any question you ask with a full sentence in reply. At first this may be difficult, but once the habit is developed, the words will come more easily, and the thoughts as well.

You may also have a socializing time, during the day, preferably in the afternoon, when the children are permitted to talk to one another. (If you observe carefully, you will notice the girls usually chatter away, but the boys far less so.) This situation should, of course, be kept under control. No shouting or loud talking is acceptable.

If you have children in your class who do not speak, try to encourage them to do so—by assigning such simple discussions as "Show and Tell," in which they bring in objects and talk about them, or "My favorite ...." This may be my favorite anything—sport, television program, place, food, radio program, record, song, occupation, person, pet, or book. But get these nonverbal individuals to use words. They truly need the practice.

Many youngsters enjoy having their voices recorded on tape.

However, never, never force a child to take part in any activity if he finds it distasteful. On the contrary, we have found this technique to be excellent, and have said, "If you don't cooperate, we won't let you tape your voice." The activity had become a reward in itself. Rarely have children refused to take part.

Reading Aloud!

To give your children experiences in listening, read aloud to them. The clue here is your choice of material, for they will listen to that which is stimulating and exciting, but not bother if the material is dull or uninspired. Read a ghost story, dramatizing it to the best of your ability, and they will strain to hear you. One of the favorites for older children is "The Monkey's Paw." For younger ones, they may enjoy the Dr. Doolittle stories. Do not consider this a nonfruitful use of your time or the children's. It is most valuable, and at the same time, pleasant.

Play Records

There are many types of records you can play for the purpose of training your children to listen. Some are storytelling, while others can be of events such as the first heart transplant. Bird calls and animal sounds are useful, if you get the children to attempt to differentiate between the sources.

Analyzing the Children's Speech

With older, more verbal children, you may wish to analyze their speech. Have each child read a selection and tape-record it. Then play back the tape for the entire class to discuss. Before you have the actual discussion, stress with the children the danger of a child being hurt by what is said, and make sure that every child realizes the purpose of the lesson. Then analyze each child's speech. Does anyone say, "axed instead of asked," "gonna instead of going to," or "berl instead of boil"? Make certain the criticisms are carried on in an objective manner—and warn the class beforehand that anyone who is cruel will not be permitted to record. This generally is discipline enough to get all of the children to cooperate. Save these tapes and tell the children you will be doing this again.

Tape Recording and Replay

Retape each child's voice, about six months later, and then replay the old along with the new to see if there is improvement in the child's speech.

Teach Your Children to Speak on the Telephone

Very often children have difficulty speaking on the telephone. Use two cups for phones, separating them with a long cord. Put one child on one side of the room, another on the other, and place a screen between the two. Then have one "phone" the other and describe a humorous incident such as a clown act in the circus. The object is to make the children express themselves through the use of words, without gestures.

You may wish to include a short lesson instructing the children in how to carry on a conversation:

"Hello, this is Jim speaking. May I talk to Bob, please."

"Hello, Bob, how are you? I'm fine" (or *I'm so-so, or I'm not feeling so well today*).

"I'm calling you because–" (*and launch into the main part of the conversation*).

(*At the end*) "Good-bye, Bob. I'll talk to you again."

You will find this a great help, at the beginning, for like so many other things, we take it for granted that a child knows how to carry on a conversation—and he may not. We had the pleasure of having a 12-year-old thank us for this, saying, "I didn't know how to make a phone call. I hated to. Thanks."

Assign Specific Radio Broadcasts

In this era of television, the radio is often ignored. Yet listening to it is an experience our children should have. Assign specific questions and have the children listen to certain programs to determine the answers. Choose programs which include persons with fine speech, if possible.

On-the-Spot Playlets

Assign topics and have the children prepare a playlet—by deciding themselves what they will say, and then acting it out. Do this with children who seem to be reluctant to speak, who need the practice. If they do well, praise them lavishly—for this will make them more comfortable and build their self-image. It has been our observation that many children (certainly not all), who do not speak well, suffer from a lack of self-confidence. If you can decrease or eliminate this lack of confidence, you do a great deal to help the nonverbal child. In assigning topics, choose one the child is familiar with. Some topics you might consider are:

- A decision to go swimming. (One child doesn't want to go and the other persuades him to go.)
- How to train a dog, a cat, or a parakeet.
- How to buy something in a store (involving asking for it).

94

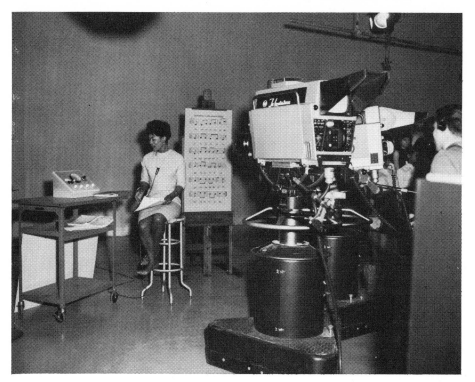

Official Photograph—Board of Education, City of N.Y

Figure 5-1

- Imagine yourself to be:
  A pitcher pitching a no-hit ball game.
  A movie star about to receive an Oscar.
  A boy getting a bicycle he has always wanted, or a girl getting a doll she has fallen in love with.

You may use these topics, or similar ones, for speeches instead of playlets. The purpose is the same, giving the child the experience of speaking to his class.

"Buzz" Sessions

Divide your class into groups. Five to six children per group is good. Then have your "Buzz" group engage in discussions. These are used very effectively in social studies to encourage the participation of as many children as possible. Not only do they do this, but they foster communication between the children. Assign topics they will enjoy, set a time limit, and have them discuss as many aspects of the topic as possible. You may wish to have the children suggest topics. For example, ten-year-old girls love horses and horse stories, and this topic would stimulate much discussion among them. Current events, if exciting, are excellent. Even gripe sessions are worthwhile—if they bring forth animated communication. Have one child in each group act as the secretary, take notes, and then report the results to the entire class.

Comparing Speech from Various Parts of Our Country

Speech variations are interesting, and making comparisons is worth the effort, particularly if you have children in your classes displaying some of the various sectional speech patterns. Tapes of television and radio broadcasts, and other recordings, can supply you with many others. This is training in listening.

If any child does not speak clearly, try to help him clarify his enunciation. Do not, however, embarrass him. Work with him while the other children are busy with other assignments.

READING

As every teacher knows, the ability to read is the main dictator of success in school. Without it a child is doomed to failure. We are not including methods for teaching reading in this volume—but since we believe a child becomes more proficient with practice, we are listing techniques which will give him experiences in reading in a number of different situations.

Write Your Own Material

Move away from simple reading material as soon as possible.

Children are naturally inquisitive, curious individuals, and we can think of few devices which will kill this curiosity more quickly than some of the fundamental reading matter. We suggest you determine your children's interests and rexograph materials they will enjoy. A child will read amusing anecdotes with far more relish than insipid tales of everyday life. Try mystery or drama, too, for a change of pace.

We have often felt our children's intelligence actually being insulted by some of the drills they are given. Why should a child try to read dull, drab sentences? Why not "See the cowboy," "There is a storm coming," or "The siren is blowing," "The firetruck is rushing down the street."

If you are willing to prepare materials such as these, we are sure you will find your children recognizing words far more quickly. They have shown they learn "elephant" more easily than "that," because of the ease with which they can visualize the animal. Of course, they must learn "that," too, but they will do so far more quickly in an exciting context.

Games

Anything made into a game is attractive. It can add excitement to a class, and serves as a motivator as well. Starting with the old-fashioned spelling bee, there are many variations you can develop. For example, the following, for word recognition.

Distribute pieces of oaktag, about 1 foot long and 6 inches high. Have the children print words on them—the vocabulary words you are teaching. Make sure they are correct. Use crayons, so the words are visible from a distance. If each child prints ten different words, you have approximately 300 to work with.

Line the children up by teams—boys against girls, or any grouping you choose. Show a word. The child must read it correctly or he is out. When the first child is out, he can show the cards. The second one out becomes scorekeeper. Keep this up for a specific length of time until one team wins.

On a corner of your board, or on a chart, keep track of the winners. You may wish to give them a decal or sticker of some sort to indicate their superiority.

Word Recognition Through Signs

If you place printed material (large letters) around your room— charts, posters, etc.—your children will read this. Such words as "Exit," "Entrance," "Emergency," "Police," "Fire," should be as familiar to them as their names. Reading names is fun, too, and you can make a large seating chart (at least 3 feet wide) which you hang on the board or wall. The children will associate the word with the name of the child. If you explain that many teachers use this kind of chart, too, they will be impressed by it.

Open-End Stories

Put your children into a story by using this device. Rexograph a short story, leaving the ending to the child's imagination. For example, you might have him stranded in a strange city, lost on a desert island, or being chased by a lion. The children will be motivated to read the story because they are in it. If any of the vocabulary is unfamiliar to them, teach it before they read the story. Be imaginative—girls will become airline stewardesses or movie stars; boys change into baseball players, cowboys, or possibly the President of the United States. They will read even difficult words under these circumstances. Repeat the vocabulary, though, on future occasions, or they will not retain it.

Timely Reading Material

Everyone needs to read a newspaper. Do it in school. Make sure your children know how to look for news, for features, for columns, and for the comics. Even first graders can benefit by "reading" a newspaper.

Encourage the reading of magazines as well. Use them as supplemental material. When articles are particularly important, it is possible to duplicate them for the entire class.

Provide your children with experiences in reading many different types of publications. Even the picture variety contain much reading matter.

Keep magazines in your classroom, and encourage your children to read them when they have completed the work assigned. Use those geared to young people—and to adults. We would suggest, though, that you review each magazine for its suitability.

If your school has a publication, use this as a basis for some reading lessons. We have found children enjoy reading the work of their predecessors, and these serve as motivational devices for the writing of stories and poems as well.

Reading Plays and Scripts of Broadcasts

Many times it is more interesting to read a play than a story. Select portions which are stimulating—it is often not necessary to read the entire play. Comedies, too, are excellent for this purpose. Conversation is more easily read than narrative writing. If you can obtain scripts from radio or television broadcasts, these, too, are exciting.

This work may be the nucleus for assembly programs. If a play requires too much memorization, it can always be "read" as a radio broadcast.

Choral Speaking

This activity combines reading with speaking and is good experience in each. It is an excellent classroom activity—but, here, too, choice of material is important. Above all, avoid the singsong type of speech which is so prevalent when children read poetry.

Some of Robert Louis Stevenson's poems are excellent for this, and you might try "The Highwayman" as well. Parts of *Alice in Wonderland* or *Old Yeller* are worth experimenting with. You may have several children read certain lines, and the rest of the group the balance of the selection.

Reading Labels, Instruction Booklets, and Guarantees

More and more of the equipment purchased in the home comes accompanied by guarantees and/or instruction booklets. Your children should be familiar with some of the more difficult words and the concepts behind them. This can be very helpful in homes where little or no English is spoken, and in the future when the boys and girls have their own homes.

Have your children read the labels on all varieties of things—to check for ingredients and for poisonous effects. Young children should be taught to recognize the skull and crossbones indicating "Poison," as soon as possible. This makes a very dramatic lesson, one they will enjoy. Bring in a bottle of Tincture of Iodine, and your lesson is motivated, as they observe the diagram and read the words.

Class Library

Encourage your children to bring into class the books they have enjoyed reading, so that their classmates may share them. The parents may wish to contribute books, if they are requested to do so, but they should be "pupil tested." Such favorites as *Charlotte's Web*, by E. B. White, will encourage the boys and girls to use reading as a source of entertainment. Help them discover the fun books offer to them, the companionship they may find, and the worlds books open for the avid reader.

The Book Race

There are those individuals who frown on competition. Perhaps each of us has some conflict about it. But we do know that setting

Official Photograph—Board of Education, City of N.Y

Figure 5-2

100

up a competitive situation does encourage many children, and we personally have seen sixth graders read more than 150 books in a ten-month school year—books of many varieties and of every length.

Posting a large chart, on which the name of every child in the class was listed, and crediting each as a book was completed (this was ascertained by class discussion and a single-paragraph report), served as an excellent device for motivation; particularly with bright children. The teacher gave the child a square to paste next to his name after he had completed a book. The color of the square indicated the area—biography, science, mystery, adventure, anthology, or poetry.

At the end of the year, a prize was given—of course it was a book.

Exchanging Books

Books, particularly paperbacks, are sometimes so relatively inexpensive that an exchange is fine. Set up a corner of your room where this may take place and encourage it. Books will probably be traded by members of the same sex, since the range of interests is most often shared by other girls or by other boys.

Book Salesmen

After children have read books they enjoyed, encourage them to "sell" them to their classmates by telling them something of the story—but not "giving it away." They may even read bits to the class. This form of book report is fun and of value.

Amateur Little-Theatre Groups

Divide your class into groups. Rexograph a play and have each group work on the same play. Make sure every child has the experience of taking part in it. Then present each group to the rest of the class. After all are presented, have the children select one group to do the play for the assembly. Or, if several performances are scheduled, permit each group to do one.

Be sure no child is ever embarrassed or denigrated for his performance.

For each group pick one director, or you will find this activity too taxing for you. Give the children instructions and then allow the director to do the rest.

Research, in Your Classroom or the Library

You can pose problems for the children to solve and have them work on this in class. You will need books covering the subject and encyclopedias, atlases, dictionaries, or the children may be taken to the library. This type of work is done well in committees, which are valuable because they train children to work together—a skill which is absolutely essential for success in living.

Choose topics of interest to the children and those for which they will be able to find relevant material. Be sure the topics are broad enough to have much available data.

WRITING

Handwriting

We find one of the most fundamental lessons is often forgotten today. Children are not taught to sign their names, and yet this is something they need to do all their lives. Please teach your children to write their names and addresses legibly. We all know about signing checks with X's, but in the era of compulsory education, shouldn't every child be able to identify himself by a clear signature?

Far from downgrading penmanship, we believe there is a need for it, and suggest that when you teach a child, you must include as one of your objectives, the ability to physically write.

The Picture Dictionary

The "picture" dictionary is an excellent introduction to writing, and the use of the dictionary. Most important, it is one which the children enjoy.

Distribute six sheets of drawing paper to each child. Fold them in half, and have available colored string to tie the pages together. They may be tied without making holes, or, if you desire, with two holes on the side or the top.

Allow the children to be creative in designing the cover, and the entire book. You may be very much surprised by the ingenuity of even the little first graders. One of my children had drawn a picture

102

of an open book with the words tumbling out. Above it he printed, "My Picture Dictionary."

For the first year, the first page would consist of a large letter "A, a" with the words "An apple" written on top, and, of course, a colorful picture of an apple. "B, b" with a banana; "C, c"—carrot or cat, corn or candy.

In the second year, the children's words may be used at the bottom of the page in a sentence. The book may be illustrated with montages, a combination of drawings and pictures cut out of magazines and old books. (Be sure to use the scissors made specifically for children to avoid possible accidents.)

If there should be non-English speaking children in the school, an excellent gesture of welcome and sharing intellectual treasures would be for the children who have made these dictionaries to present them to the children learning our language.

Making Up and/or Doing Crossword Puzzles

Both the construction and the working of a crossword puzzle have benefits. They utilize vocabulary and give the child the desire to learn a greater number of words, and words of a more complex nature. Start with simple puzzles, which your children will be able to do and which offer them gratification, and then go on to more complicated ones.

Playing Scrabble is worthwhile, too, for the same reasons.

When the children construct puzzles, do not make it necessary for every box to be filled in, since this is very difficult. A puzzle might look like this:

C	O	O	P	E	R	A	T	E
A	M		E		E			Y
M	E	N	T		M			E
E	N	T	R	A	N	C	E	S
R			O		A	H		
A	T		L	O	N	E	R	
			E	N	T	A	I	L
T	O		U			T	O	
O	F		M				T	

Writing Books for Younger Children

Starting with second or third graders, you can have your children write books for their little brothers or sisters. Use the same type of folded pages suggested for the picture dictionary.

You may find it necessary to give the children suggestions at the beginning, and have them copy them from the board and illustrate them. As you go on, however, you will find your children able to offer many ideas of their own.

The books prepared should be presented to the younger children, with ceremony, and both groups will be pleased.

Contest Entries

Contest entries often call for compositions or themes.

Winning prizes is worth striving for, and your children should be

Figure 5-3

given the opportunity to compete for such prizes whenever the occasion is announced. Writing such compositions is good training and presents a reason for writing. However, before the children start to write, discuss the topic. Give them ideas, so they have something to say. You will find they will think of many others, if you have gotten them started, for thought begets thought. Fire Prevention Week, for example, is often commemorated by an essay contest.

Write a Textbook

Very often children do research and accumulate enough material to write a textbook of their own. This can have much value. They are writing with a purpose, and if you tell them you plan to submit their work to a publisher, they will be motivated still more. We know of one teacher who did this and have seen the fine textbook which resulted. Some topics you might use are:

- Famous people of our city. (Each child is responsible for one person, or you may have a committee of two per celebrity.)
- Famous baseball players. (Would girls be interested?)
- Famous artists (after a trip to a museum of art).

You could then use postcard reproductions in the book. Make one copy of the book, or, if possible, rexograph a copy for each child. Insist upon perfection, explaining that this is a textbook—and when it is completed, submit it to a publisher.

Letter Writing

Give your children experiences in writing letters—but have them write real letters:

- To pen pals in foreign lands, other states, or cities within our country.
- To the consulates of foreign nations, for information concerning their countries.
- To friends, inviting them to visit.
- To large corporations for the free materials issued by their Public Relations Departments. (Many school libraries have books listing such firms, with indications of their offerings—and there is an absolutely huge variety.)
- To friends who are ill, or to people who are shut-ins.

You may wish to start this letter writing by asking the child to write to you, giving you some information about himself. Tell him to include any material he wishes to, and nothing he'd rather omit. Give the class some ideas, such as, "My life at home," or "My pets," "My favorite people," "My interests." Be sure you tell the children these letters are personal communications between them and you, and that they are highly confidential. You might give them a letter from you to serve as a model. It might read:

Dear Barbara,

    I am very happy to welcome you to class 5-361. I have been teaching in this school for four years, and I believe your brother, Joseph, was one of my pupils. . .

This is time consuming, but your children will treasure this letter—and you will gain immeasurably from the rapport it can engender.

Writing Compositions

Base your compositions on your children's experiences. For example, take them on trips and have them write about them. These excursions should be stimulating, and should be chosen with this in mind.

A movie like "The Heart Is a Lonely Hunter," a play such as *Wait Until Dark*, a concert by James Brown, a visit to a zoo or aquarium, a flight in a jet plane or a helicopter, a ferryboat ride, a performance of *Hamlet*, or a rodeo—the variety of experiences you may offer is tremendous.

When you return to class, discuss the trip—and then ask your children to write a composition related to it in some way. Perhaps a person in the play interested them, or an animal at the zoo. Perhaps it was their reaction to the situation—the problem in the pit of their stomachs as the plane circled or the boat tossed. But use the experience as a basis for the composition.

Compiling a Book of Class Humor

This assignment can really be lots of fun. Have each child write a funny story which will be included in the book. We suggest the teacher contribute some of her own, as well. Use a scrapbook, pasting each story on a page. If you have a parent available who can type the stories, you can have this done on rexograph and distribute it to the children.

Here are some examples:

A man walked up to a woman with a carrot in her ear. "Pardon me, Miss," he said, "But you have a carrot in your ear."
She turned to him and said, "What?"
"You have a carrot in your ear."
"What? I can't hear you."
He repeated patiently, "You have a carrot in your ear."
"I'm sorry," she said, "I can't hear you. I have a carrot in my ear."

Or the little girl who went up to her teacher and asked, "Who is Richard Sands?"
The teacher stopped, thought for a moment. "Where did you hear the name?" she asked.
"We say it every day," the child answered.
"Do we?" Now the teacher was really perplexed. "When?"
"You know," the girl replied, "I pledge allegiance to the flag of the United States of America, and to the republic for Richard Sands."

Letters to the Editor

When there are current issues of interest to your children, it is worthwhile, after a discussion in the classroom, to have the children write letters to the editor of the local newspaper. Such letters are often printed, which makes the effort worthwhile. Even if they are not, teaching the children that they can present their opinions, and the manner in which to present them, is very important.

Guess Who?

Have your children write one-paragraph profiles describing people—people they know or famous personalities. Then have them read them to the class without giving the name, and have the children try to determine who is being described.

Start by writing and reading a paragraph of your own. We once did such a profile of Charley Brown, Snoopy's friend. The children loved it and wrote fine profiles of their own.

Trips

There is a long list of possible trips associated with the teaching of language arts. Let us begin with the library—which should be introduced to every first grader. By taking the children there, making them feel comfortable, and encouraging them to get library cards, you start them on the path to reading on their own.

Newspaper offices, moving pictures, and the theatre are other possibilities. Try to think, too, of the unusual, the dramatic.

One of the best poetry lessons we ever observed was the time a friend, to commemorate the birthday of Edgar Allen Poe, took us to Poe's Cottage. There, on the lawn, near the little house, were children listening to their teacher reciting "Annabel Lee" with beauty and fervor. These children were not bored for a moment. They were learning to appreciate poetry while their bodies were relaxed in the sunshine, unconfined to any seat or desk in the classroom. Can you take your children to visit the home of a famous author? Washington Irving's house, Sunnyside, at Tarrytown, N.Y. is a joy. As we have mentioned before, any trip may be a valuable experience linked to the study of the language arts.

Safety Plays

Since safety is extremely important, why not have your children write plays which may be presented to students in the lower grades? These may include songs as well.

The Clinic

Establish a "clinic" for reading or writing. Have the bright children work with the slower ones—or tutor boys and girls in other classes, or children in a lower grade.

If you decide to do this, be sure no child feels offended. Perhaps a boy who needs help in reading can teach his "teacher" to hit a baseball. Work with the "teachers," explaining to them exactly what they are to do—and be sure they understand.

Television

This most modern medium gives our children the opportunity to have truly amazing experiences. It intriguingly offers us the chance to meet the leaders of the world, face-to-face, and we are able to partake in national and world affairs, which were once considered to be the business of the diplomat and the statesman. There is a series of phonograph records, called, "You Are There," which make the listener feel he is at the scene. But with television you really are there.

There is a saying which goes, "If you can't beat 'em, join 'em." We cannot beat television, much as we might wish to—sometimes. Let us join it—by careful selection—and let us make it one of our tools, for it lends itself to being an extremely important one. The key word here is selection. Select, and having done this carefully, advise your pupils.

Each Sunday the newspapers print listings of the programs for the coming week. Why not read through them, and determine which programs are applicable to the subjects you are teaching? List these, and offer credit for pupils who watch them, and then make reports. An even better method is to set up a television committee, whose task it is to check Sunday's paper and prepare listings for their classmates, of presentations which would be of value to them. In this case, do not limit the listings to your particular topics, topics which are being studied at the present time. If the children realize a Shakespearean play is being presented, some may wish to watch it, and so it should be included, regardless of specific subject, for one way in which our children may become familiar with some of the best English and American literature is to see it dramatized; this is often done very effectively on television. What more beautiful play can we show than Sir Lawrence Olivier's *Hamlet*? There are science programs of exceptional value, such as "The Birth of a Child"; actually the variety from which to select the best is unlimited.

It is certainly one of our tasks, as teachers, to inform pupils of these offerings and encourage them to choose programs which have educational value. One seventh-grade pupil said, "I watched a program about the birth of a child (mentioned above), and decided right then to become a doctor." Will he? Who can tell? But he was inspired by the experience and surely this is important.

To make sure your pupils participate actively, give them an assignment to do. You may have them write a summary, answer questions, or be prepared to discuss the program.

In certain localities, there are special television stations which telecast only educational material. You may wish to subscribe to the program guides they publish, for very often the type of program you would like to work into your lesson is shown and listed therein.

Perhaps you will find it necessary to set up criteria with your children. If you feel they have not learned to be critical in regard to some of the material shown, discuss this with them—but have *them* set up the criteria, don't *tell* them. In fact, encourage them to tell you. We do not mean to imply that there is anything wrong with watching ball games or a golf match. We do feel, though, that cartoons should be limited; however, in many households this particular type of viewing is indulged in every Saturday morning. As the teacher, here, again, it is your task to guide, not to tell the children what to do.

Politicians have discovered the importance of this medium, and your pupils should be encouraged to take an active part in the campaigns, if only by listening to the candidates and watching them speak. Never in the history of the world have we been so close to a battlefield as we are to the war in Vietnam or to some of the rioting in the streets. Here, too, it is possible for boys and girls to get firsthand experiences through the eyes of the cameraman. The children need our help, however, in making interpretations of what they see.

Your class may enjoy watching "College Bowl" and the lower-school level equivalent. Here boys and girls are given a chance to excel because of their academic knowledge. The questions are sometimes easy enough for your students to get a few correct. This is good ego building and the children are able to identify with the youngsters on the screen. Other quiz shows, while not to be specifically recommended, should not be scorned, either.

If your school has a television set among the audio-visual aids available, you may find programs televised which you will be able to view with your students. These might include news broadcasts and commentaries on current events, travel programs, visits to industrial plants.

110

Try to choose those programs which will hold the students' interest. If you have a television lesson, be sure to give an assignment, so that the pupils are viewing the program with a purpose. Such assignments might include:

- A summary of the program, bringing out the important points covered.
- Note taking, which is valuable because the children will be interested in giving their opinions to one another in regard to the program.
- Using the information given by the program to have a debate, subsequently, or a panel discussion.

The more ingenious your assignment, the more the class will enjoy the program.

It is very possible that there will be a telecast which you will wish to recommend to your classes which will require some advance preparation. For example, if the class was asked to view "Elizabeth the Queen," you might wish to discuss Elizabethan England, the customs, and the background of the times. You could inject information in regard to Elizabeth's father, the infamous Henry VIII, and her mother, Anne Boleyn. This type of preparation would be particularly important with Shakespearean plays, for when one knows something of the period and the mores, the play is far more interesting. With scientific offerings, if lessons are needed to cover the fundamental understandings, make sure you give these before the program is viewed by your classes.

An interview program may be so affecting an experience that you and your pupils might react as the gentleman who said to me, "I was at a party and someone, a Negro, was telling me about the humiliation he had suffered while traveling." Then the man laughed, and said, "Oh, no. It was an interview with Sammy Davis on television." This gentleman had actually felt he had met and talked with this famous entertainer.

Many of the informal discussion programs, such as David Susskind's "Open End," have this effect. The audience often feels it actually participates in the discussion. Perhaps this might be a bridge which might connect television and our classrooms in timely controversies.

Let us, by all means, be careful in our selection of such programs, choosing those which are democratic, high-minded, and a tribute to ourselves and to our country.

During his term in office, President Franklin D. Roosevelt initiated a series of radio talks, which he called "Fireside Chats." He used them to become close to the American people. They were quite effective, but television is even more so. The more recent Presidents' faces are as familiar to us, and should be, as family friends. When the President speaks to us, we can see his expression and his emotion. Shouldn't we encourage our students to watch such speeches, to see our executives "in action" and really learn to know them?

Folk singing, one of the parents of rock and roll, can be enjoyed by your pupils. Pete Seeger, for example, comments on current and bygone days, giving us insight into the building of our nation. Donovan brings music from lands all over the world—hoping to bring us, as human beings, closer together, by showing us a little more about the culture of others. Charity Bailey and Buffy St. Marie, the American Indian entertainer, have appeared on television. Wouldn't it broaden the vision of the children, and increase their interest in their brothers and sisters in other lands, by singing the songs themselves in school after having enjoyed them on the screen at home? They may have seen and heard Harry Belafonte bringing us the joyous music of Israel as he sings "Hava Negilah." How stirring is Mahalia Jackson singing Negro spirituals, and also Andy Williams' version of "Dominique." Isn't the use of folk songs one of the most charming and enjoyable ways of bringing our children closer to the children of other lands, and of giving them the opportunities to experience musical expressions from the entire world?

Some of the most magnificent music in the world is presented on television. If your students seem to be ready for experiencing classical, orchestral music, why not recommend a televised concert? But a word of caution! Prepare them for this experience by telling them, as specifically as you can, what to listen for. Do not suggest a program which is too long, or too complex, nor one which would appeal only to the sophisticated concert-goer. Suit the program to the needs of the children. Musical plays, too, such as "Finian's Rainbow" or "Brigadoon" are wonderful introductions to the music of the theatre, and are occasionally offered to the television audience.

You may wish to use a television program to motivate a lesson. Certainly almost any of those mentioned might be utilized in just that way. If you will use your skill in questioning, you can develop fascinating lessons in this manner. There is one pitfall, however; this should be done only if the program may be viewed in school, because it would be unfair to children who might not be able to view it, if you assigned a program to be seen at home.

We have still another task in regard to the use of this modern medium. We must try to negate the bloodthirsty experiences which are shown. There are pupils, especially boys, who will, if given their choice, view little else. Indeed, even on the news broadcasts the violence shown is, at times, frightening. In our classrooms, should we not point out that these are the things which "make news"? Somewhere in our teaching, we must help our children realize the actual horrors of violence of any kind. In the one hour the clergyman may have per week, he can hardly complete the task of teaching, "Thou shalt not commit any act or deed which will hurt thy brother." He needs, and must have, our help.

Try to show your boys and girls that, while laws outlawing capital punishment have been passed in a great many states, violence is still prevalent in our land, and we sometimes actually witness it through the medium of television. Within the year 1968 we saw the funerals of not one, but two assassinated leaders, men who had dedicated their lives to aiding the poor, the downtrodden of our land.

The funerals of President John F. Kennedy, first, and then of Dr. Martin Luther King and Senator Robert Kennedy were filled with honor and glory. As teachers we should help the children to experience and interpret these, so that they are not so impressed with all of the honor and glory that they lose sight of the tragic loss of these young men, whose passing leaves our nation so much poorer. For many years there has been some public pressure for Congress to pass legislation prohibiting the sale of guns. Would it not be effective to have our young people become aware of this situation and discuss it? After the discussions you might suggest to them that they write to their representatives in Congress, in favor of strong legislation in this regard. It is important to give our boys and girls experiences in the actual events of the day, and there is no better way to do this than through the medium of television.

Conclusion

In this chapter, we have outlined a series of techniques which you may use to teach the four basic areas of communication—listening, speaking, writing, and reading. Because of the tremendous impact television has made upon our style of living, we have included a section on it—suggesting specific procedures you may wish to follow. In every one of these, we have stressed the activities the children do—activities involving active participation, rather than observation.

Do not shortchange your children. They need these skills more than any others in the world. The child who cannot speak well is limited in almost everything he does. The child who cannot read is severely handicapped throughout his school life and thereafter. Therefore, on behalf of every child, may we implore you—teach them to really communicate by giving them numerous and varied experiences in these areas.

• • • **6** • • •

Making an Impact
with Experiences in
Science and Math

~~~~~~~~~~~~~~~~~~~~~~~~

SCIENCE—THE EASIEST SUBJECT TO MAKE EXPERIENTIAL

Of all the major subject areas, science is probably the easiest to make experiential—for when we think of science teaching, we should think of experimentation. This may take many forms: by each child; by groups of children; by several children demonstrating to the rest; by the teacher, assisted by children; by the teacher working himself. This listing is in order of preference—because it is infinitely better to have the child work, himself, than for the teacher to do a demonstration. However, for many reasons, the former is not always feasible. But experimentation is still the key to the best science learning. This, then, will be basic to all of the methods we will suggest.

A Study of Natural Phenomena

Snow

1. (a) Have your children set up straight-edged containers on a windowsill, or in another place where they will catch the snow. After a snowfall, have them measure the amount of snow in terms of inches.

(b) Instruct them to melt the snow, by placing the jar in a warm spot. After it has melted, measure the amount of water and compare this with the amount of snow.

Surprisingly, 10 to 12 inches of snow will often yield only 1 to 1½ inches of water. This is true of dry snow. Of course, if the snow is wet, the yield is entirely different.

This experiment may be done each time it snows, and records can be kept to determine the ratio of snow to water.

2. Place some slides in a freezer or refrigerator. When you are ready to use them, remove them, place a very small amount of snow

117

on them, and have the children look at them under the microscope. The snow usually melts, but if the children are able to see snowflakes, they will long remember the experience.

3. Examine samples of snow, which appears to be clean, but which has been mixed with dirt from air or other pollutants, under the microscope.

4. Have the children review the importance of snow in terms of the commerce and daily activities of their community to show them how important it can be—how much money may be lost by businesses as a result of a storm. For example, have them ask their parents how they were affected by the last snowstorm. Then move on to the importance of snow in terms of agriculture and drought.

5. (a) Why does it sometimes take snow a long time to melt? Have children take samples of snow and keep them at various temperatures. Remember to discuss the quantity they are using. Explain the concept of melting—that it requires more heat to melt snow on the street than in the test tube.

(b) Add rock salt to the melting snow and have the children note the result. Have them explain the outcome.

Freezing of Water

1. Does salt water really freeze? Experiment by having the children make up solutions of varying concentrations. Have them fill test tubes to the very top, seal, and place in a heavy plastic bag. Next, put them in a freezer. What are the results? Why? Be sure to include one test tube full of plain water, which would be frozen as well, to act as a control.

2. If there is ice-skating in your community, have the children find out how thick the ice must be before they are permitted to skate on it. Appoint a committee to investigate.

3. What happens to fish in lakes which freeze? Have children do research on this.

Static Electricity

The playful little electrons we call static electricity can be lots of fun, experientially.

1. Have your children, at home, stand in a darkened room and remove a synthetic sweater by pulling it off quickly. What do they see? (This experiment will work only in a dry atmosphere.)

2. Tear up pieces of paper into confetti and have some placed on each desk. Then have each child run a comb quickly through his hair, and hold the comb, horizontally, about an inch above the confetti. If

the child's hair is clean and dry, it will generously give off electrons, the comb will become charged, and it will attract the paper. This experiment, however, will not always work unless the conditions are right. But it is a good teaching device, nevertheless, and one worth having the children try.

3. Mix salt and pepper, and place the mixture on a sheet of paper. Comb the hair, in the same manner as described above, and hold the comb over the mixture, at a height of 1 inch. If the experiment works, only one of the components of the mixture is attracted; it is fun to see the grains jump up to the comb.

When studying any natural phenomenon, have the children try to explain when, where, and above all, why it happens.

Writing Up Experiments

Children need experience in keeping records of their work. Each experiment they do should be written up as part of their science notebook. We suggest you use the following form: Problem, Method, Observation, Conclusion. This is concise, to the point, yet inclusive enough to help the child recall any experiment. For example:

Problem: *What do living cells look like under the microscope?*
Method: *Scrape the inside of your cheek with a sterile stick. Rub the side of the stick, rather than the tip, on the inner, upper surface of your mouth. Next, rub it gently on a slide. Place this on the microscope stage and examine it under low and high power.*
Observation: *The cells, under low power, looked like this: (Draw a clear diagram, about 2 inches in size.)*
Conclusion: *The cheek cells I saw have a rectangular shape. They appeared slightly irregular because we scraped them, and probably we broke some of them as we removed them.*

Train your children to write up every experiment they do—and the demonstration lessons, as well. However, be sure you review their work with them, stressing the basic concepts.

Experiments done at home should be written up in the same manner. The notebooks must be neat and the diagrams correct. It is a grave error to accept poor work from any child, at any time. If need be, work should be rewritten—stressing the need for perfect or near-perfect achievement. By accepting work of poor quality, you cheat the children, for they never learn the psychological rewards of a well-performed task.

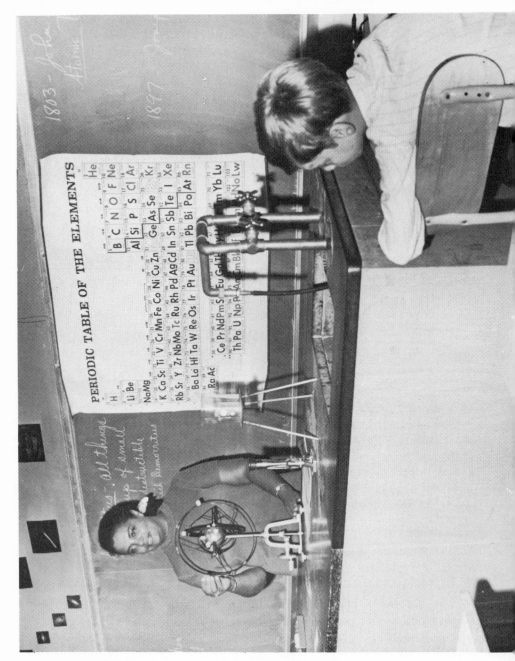

Official Photograph—Board of Education, City of N.Y

Figure 6-1

Construction of Working Models

When you teach a scientific principle, if possible, have your children make models, toys, or instruments to explain it.

Children have successfully built steam engines, pinhole cameras, crystal radios, electric motors—and countless other devices. Toys such as matching games, burglar alarms, or those using the principle of the electromagnet are easily constructed.

When a child takes the trouble to construct a device, be sure you discuss it with him to be sure he understands the scientific concept behind it. Then commend him and give him credit for doing it. Reinforce the experiences, too, by having each child explain his work to the class, and exhibit it.

Children enjoy making electrical circuits or anemometers, elevators or levers, water purification systems or model cities. It is our task to help them discover their interests and apply them.

Growing Things

Encourage your children to grow plants of all varieties at home, as well as in the classroom: from seeds, from bulbs, from cuttings, from roots—sweet potatoes, carrot tops, avocado pits—the list is truly endless. There are unusual plants which will attract attention and fascinate the children—such as the prayer plant, which folds its leaves at night.

Conduct Experiments by Changing Conditions

1. Compare plants grown in the sunlight and in shade.
2. Watch the growth of stems toward the sun or another source of light.
3. Try a variety of fertilizers. Have the children ask their parents for suggestions. We've been told to use coffee grounds, ground up eggshells, and even ground fish. (The latter is definitely not for the class with children who have sensitive noses.)

In one of my eighth grade classes the children were carrying out this kind of experimentation. They were growing a variety of plants, and using many different fertilizers. The pots with the growing plants were placed on the windowsills, labeled with the name of both the plant and the fertilizer. One little boy looked at one of the pots, marked "Birdseed" in large letters and "eggshells" in smaller ones.

121

He turned and said to his friend, "She's gone nuts, I think. She's trying to grow birds from seeds, and she's feeding them eggshells."

4. Try experiments varying the quantity of water given to the plants.

Hydroponics—Growing Plants Without Soil

This branch of agriculture may prove to be very important in the future, as it becomes more and more difficult to feed the population of the world. Plants will often grow very nicely in water, without soil, and it is possible to have a "soilless garden." Chemicals are added to the water in which the plants are grown. We have seen this experiment done very effectively, in the classroom, with tomato plants.

Have your children do the research to find out which chemicals are to be used. Have them do the measuring and weighing whenever possible. (Sometimes this is impractical because the quantities of salts, for example, which are to be used, are so minute.) Also, be sure the

Official Photograph—Board of Education, City of N.Y

Figure 6-2

light conditions are as close to perfect as you can get them, and that the temperature is as even as possible.

Miniature Greenhouses

You may wish to have the children construct their own greenhouses, using wooden boxes with one side made of glass, and with fluorescent lighting. With this controlled environment, it is possible to grow tropical plants such as cacti or orchids; other magnificent plants such as begonias do very well, too, under these conditions.

Doing the Planting for the School

Many schools have small areas outside the building which may be used for gardening. Have the children select the flowers, purchase the seeds, and do all of the work involved in gardening. There may be window boxes which they are able to plant and take care of, as well. For city children, this type of experience is very valuable.

Eliminating Superstitions

One objective of good science teaching is the elimination of superstition. An interesting way to study this area is through interviewing. Have your children interview their grandparents, and any other senior citizens, asking a series of specific questions, such as the following: What remedies did your parents or grandparents use—other than drugs or medicines? (The use of herbs, for instance, was prevalent. My father told of an old Hungarian peasant woman who used bread mold to cure infections. Was this superstition or science? Penicillin, of course, is derived from the molds grown on bread, and so it appears she was using penicillin almost half a century ago. However, I remember, too, that a piece of camphor was worn around the neck to ward off poliomyelitis. This was absolutely useless, and an excellent example of superstition.)

Other questions: Why do we knock on wood? (To ward off the evil spirits.)

Why do we say, "God bless you," when someone sneezes?

What about the Irish leprechauns? And the poltergeists of today?

Have the children list the most common superstitions—i.e. a black cat crossing one's path, opening an umbrella in the house. Have them research to find out how they started, and why there are people who believe in them.

Trips to Supply Experiences

There are some topics in the study of science which are difficult to make experiential. However, a trip to the planetarium should be substituted for the textbook when studying astronomy. In discussing the possibility of life on other planets, encourage the reading of science fiction. H. G. Wells, Jules Verne, and other authors of yesteryear are as exciting as those of today in this area.

Wouldn't taking a ride in a jet-propelled plane teach more about aircraft and jet propulsion than any other way? Or, if that is not possible, why not a trip to an airport to watch the planes landing and taking off? Can you arrange a visit to the control tower? Just picture how your class would react to that.

Trips to museums of natural history, to zoological and botanical gardens, to fish hatcheries or game preserves, to large factories or assembly plants, water purification centers or weather bureaus—these are all possibilities. For city children, should they not, as a most important part of their education, see cows, horses, chickens, and ducks? Perhaps a trip to a farm would be in order. We know of one little girl who thought they *made* milk at the bottling plant near her home.

Studying the Individual

Each of us is fundamentally interested in himself. Why not put your children right into your science program? In using a microscope, for example, have them study the dirt under their nails, the cells from their cheeks, and the root tips from their own hair.

Have them take their own pulses, before and after doing exercises, and have them feel their own hearts beating. Teach them to test for the knee-jerk reflex, and for the Babinski reflex reaction. Using mirrors, they can study the pupils of their eyes as they react to changes in light intensity.

Astrology is interesting and very related to the individual—his exact time and place of birth. Instruct the children to do research to find out whether it is actually scientific or not. Choose a series of dates and check them against various horoscopes. Call attention to the statements which usually compose them. Are they really scientific?

Chemicals at Work

Chemicals make up the entire world around us. Even at an early age, children may be introduced to them. Even second graders will enjoy being taught the symbols for some of the more common elements—hydrogen (H) or oxygen (O), for example.

Photography is an excellent example of chemicals at work. Why not allow your children to take pictures, and develop and print them. A closet can be converted easily into an acceptable darkroom.

You can make vinegar, and in so doing, illustrate the fermentation process. Yogurt, too, showing bacterial processes, is easily produced. Various indicators, such as litmus paper, which change color due to differences in acidity, are interesting and enable your children to test for the presence of an acid.

In studying solutions, use common ones—such as coffee, tea, salt water—and then proceed to more complex ones. It is better learning for a child to taste lemonade and figure out what it is, than to see a colorless solution and be told it is X dissolved in Y. The effect of a silver nitrate solution on skin is interesting, but results in a long-wearing stain. Be careful. When you are teaching chemistry, it is most important that you start with known solutions, and then go on to unknown ones. Children, for instance, are familiar with tincture of iodine. Here is an example of a chemical dissolved in alcohol, rather than in water. It is also a substance with which the children are familiar.

Feeding the World

The problem of feeding the world is an extremely important one. Discuss possible solutions, such as the following:

1. We have already mentioned hydroponics.
2. Discuss the many products which may be used which come from the oceans. Have the children bring in examples of each—seaweed, shellfish, fish. Discuss the preparation of food from each of these.
3. Improved foods have been developed, such as the variety using soybeans. Have the children send to "Meals for Millions," for samples of their product, so that they may actually taste it for themselves. They may then wish to raise funds for this organization, which feeds so many people.

4. Have the children write to the United Nations for information on this topic.

5. Discuss the use of fertilization to improve food crops, and also the use of modern equipment, and what they can do to increase harvests, particularly in the underdeveloped nations.

6. Do a study of insecticides and their effect on food production.

7. It has been stated that many, many millions of people go to bed hungry every night. Let us consider approximately how much money it would require to feed these millions, and where this money could come from. Should we not, as part of our work in science, and social studies, too, awaken in our children deep feelings of compassion for the myriad of less fortunate people throughout the world?

This topic is an excellent nucleus for poster work in art, in composition, in poetry writing, and in dramatization, for it brings these problems into focus in the minds of the children.

Developing Hobbies Through Studying Science

Lifelong hobbies may be developed in the classroom. Children have become interested in such pastimes as bird-watching and gardening, and have carried these interests into their adult lives. Identifying trees, collecting and classifying rocks and fossils (particularly in those areas where they are readily found) are fascinating, and the potential geologist may be taught to study the history of an area by the markings on the surface—through rocks and natural formations. These phenomena are often found in a child's immediate surroundings. For example, Manhattan Island is rich in geologic history, showing many changes which it went through, and across the Hudson River are the Palisades, which are equally interesting.

Raising pets—such as hamsters, gerbils, tropical fish, or birds—can be taught in the classroom, and the children can benefit immeasurably if they are permitted to actually care for the animals.

Smoking and Narcotics

From the time they are very young, most of our children have been bombarded with cigarette advertising. Smoking is always pictured as pleasant and desirable. It becomes incumbent upon us to counteract this by educating the youngsters. They must learn the possible dangers of cigarette smoking—and learn them at an early age.

Start out by having each child read the warning printed on each package of cigarettes. Discuss the wording carefully, making sure the child understands every word. Have on hand models of the heart and lungs, and discuss the possible changes which might happen to these organs from excessive smoking. If you can obtain specimens from a local hospital, you may wish to show the actual tissues. We have used a bona fide cancerous lung, and have found it has had a profound effect on the children who have seen it.

Another technique to make this learning experiential is to invite a speaker to address the children. The father of one of our boys requested the opportunity to speak to the children in our school. His larynx had been removed, because it was malignant. He had been told by his physicians that this was a direct result of smoking, and he was very anxious to bring out the danger to the children by letting them hear the way he spoke; he had done remarkably well in learning an entirely new way of talking, by forcing air up through the throat. If such a person is not available, a representative of the American Cancer Society will address the group. Films, too, are useful in teaching this particular lesson—one which needs to be taught to every boy and girl. Incidentally, do not expect to reach every child in the class. If you reach only one or two, which you surely will, the lesson is worthwhile.

The problem of the illegal use of narcotics, too, is prevalent in our land, and the children hear about drugs, often while they are still very young. Forewarned is forearmed, and by teaching them just what the medicinal uses of narcotics are, and how these pain-killing chemicals have been used for entirely different purposes, we can forestall trouble in many cases. We have invited speakers from the Narcotics Bureau, who have been excellent in explaining the situation to the boys and girls. Your Police Department probably can supply similar personnel. By bringing the problem out into the open, by showing just how dangerous and addictive drug-taking is, we are able to save some of our young people, who might be tempted to try some drug—"just once." We include glue-sniffing in this area, because this is the starting point for many youngsters. Since it has caused serious brain damage, this point must be brought out—very emphatically. Again, we can't win 'em all, but we can influence a large number of our children and we should start when they are young enough to be influenced.

More Sophisticated Trips

There are an endless number of trips which a science teacher may take with his class. Surely the obvious places you have already thought of. Now, let us suggest some more unusual places:

1. A trip to the seashore to study ecology, the study of environment. Look for all of the variety of living things to be found there, and the way in which they are affected by the sea. (You may suggest the children read *The Outermost House*, by Henry Beston. This is the chronicle of one year of his life, while he lived on the beach of Eastham, Cape Cod.) Consider, too, how man may discover nature's secrets and utilize them for his own purposes. For an added treat, read aloud "The Chambered Nautilus" by Oliver Wendell Holmes.

2. Visit the nearby countryside to study the geology of the area, encouraging the children to take their cameras to make a permanent record of their trips. Look for trees growing out of rocks, for termite nests, and for signs of rockslides and erosion.

3. Take your young children to visit a pet shop—they will absolutely adore the young animals—the baby chicks, the puppies, the kittens. They will lose their hearts to baby monkeys. This is a wholesome way to awaken in our children a love of animals.

4. Scientifically oriented movies are well worth taking your children to see. Such productions as "2001; A Space Odyssey" or "Planet of the Apes" would delight them, and raise many interesting points for discussion and research.

5. Atomic energy plants and plants producing electric power through the use of atomic energy are fascinating. In fact, any power plant is worth visiting with your children.

6. Telephone or telegraph companies, radio or television broadcasting, ocean liners, or astronomical observatories are effective motivational devices for work to be done subsequently by the children.

7. In your own school there is a fascinating place to visit and we wonder how many teachers have thought of it. Ask the custodial engineer if he would explain to your children how the school heating plant works, and if he would permit groups to visit the boiler room. This is a trip we long remember—for its informative value—and for the novelty it presented.

8. Probably one of the trips your children will never forget is a visit to the Smithsonian Institute in Washington, D. C., where the number of scientific exhibits is vast, all inclusive, and really exciting.

9. If a child, teacher, or member of the community has set up a laboratory in his home, he might like to have the children visit. It is surely worthwhile and worth a telephone call to determine if this is possible, for it might encourage other youngsters with scientific proclivities to set up their own labs.

Caution: *The lab must be safe—so that no one is in physical danger at any time during the visit. Have the owner describe his work to the visitors, to make the visit really valuable.*

MATHEMATICS—RELATED TO THE CHILDREN'S LIVES

It is impossible to teach arithmetic without experiential learning. When a child is adding, subtracting, multiplying, dividing, or solving problems, he is working experientially. However, it is possible to make these experiences more interesting, more creative, and involve the child far more if you plan your work with his specific involvement as one of your objectives. Many of the experiences we will suggest will help you to do this. Another aspect to consider is the relationship of the child's work in school to his life outside. By relating the two closely, you make his education meaningful and practical—his experiences in the classroom of real value in terms of his daily life.

Games and Puzzles

Call it a drill, give out sheets with examples or problems—and it becomes a chore. You use the same examples in a competition, similar to a spelling bee, and an entirely different attitude is engendered. Better still, to keep every child working, try the following: Hand out the duplicated sheets, divide the class into teams (use the same teams for a month, at the end of which present token prizes), and have the children do all the problems in pencil. Have the class exchange papers, stress the need for integrity, and mark only in pen (pencils have been put away). This makes it possible to prevent any change of answers or filling in any blanks. Have each child place his last name at the bottom of the paper he marked. (This, too, is a device to encourage reliability.) Then calculate the number of points each team has earned, giving one for each correct answer.

You may vary this method, but basically it makes drilling far more pleasant—indeed it will encourage participation—for every child can contribute points—however few. (May we point out, too, that this scheme for grading can be used for every short-answer test. You will have to have a supply of pens and pencils on hand, but the hours you can save are more valuable.)

This technique will work for any grade—from the first on up—because you are able to vary the work sheets to fit the children's needs. Encourage them to prepare for the competitions at home. Here, you see, is a valid reason, for example, to learn the multiplication table. The technique can be used with sets and Venn diagrams, and any other aspect of modern math, as well. It is possible to use it with almost any class.

We feel that competition is a fact of life, and that, used judiciously, it can successfully motivate the children.

Commercial games such as Monopoly and dominoes, and card games such as Casino, use math skills and give your children reasons for learning them. Even Scrabble is valuable for little ones—because they will learn to utilize words as well as to add their points.

If you set up a game period, be sure you explain to your children they are learning to add. It sounds terrible if a child reports to his parents, "All we did in school today was play Monopoly." Far better, if he comments, "Today we learned addition by playing Monopoly."

Operating Stores, Banks, Stock Brokerages, and Even Stock Exchanges

Have you observed children at play? If so, you realize that the concept of operating a store is really a game—but it is possible to learn so much!

Have the children bring in empty cans and boxes, make cardboard models, construct shelves, and they are in business. Toy money adds to the fun. Isn't it difficult to conceive of children unable to "make change," and handle money? How can we possibly have ignored this in our teaching? A visit to a supermarket, at this point, would be of value. The manager might describe, on the children's level, how the store is operated.

As children get older, operating a bank would prove to be more interesting. Then we can have them calculate interest, determine costs of loans and mortgages, and work with the rates of exchange of foreign countries' currency. A subsequent class visit to a bank adds interest and information.

The same principle may be used to work with stocks and bonds. The daily entries of stock values in the newspapers are easily utilized.

130

Official Photograph—Board of Education, City of N.Y

Figure 6-3

Trips to a stock brokerage or the exchange will heighten the excitement, and will show the importance of arithmetic in the world scene.

Graphs may be tied in to this work, as well as decimals, fractions, and the laws of probability.

Measuring and Constructing

In teaching measurements, it is far more experiential to do the real thing than to talk about it.

1. Won't your young children enjoy learning liquid measurement by filling cups, quarts, gallons, etc. with water? Will they not learn far more by pouring four cups into a quart than by being told 4 cups = 1 quart?

And how much more fun it is if they calculate and then do the following:

A can of frozen lemonade costs 12 cents. We get 4 cups from it,

131

when the water is added. If we sell each cup for 5 cents, how much profit do we make? Try to get permission to sell candy, pretzels, or cookies in the lunchroom. Have the boys and girls do the bookkeeping, keeping track of the costs, expenses, etc.

The point is to *do* more often than to say.

2. Are you teaching linear measurements? Why not build model buildings? Use cardboard cartons, shoeboxes, even matchboxes. Have the children do all of the measuring with accuracy—windows, doors, etc. Combine this with your artwork and you have fascinated children —and fascinating displays.

Contrast the size of the Empire State Building with a steamship, and watch the children's eyes light up. Have them make scale models or drawings, and they have even more fun. Is there a park in your area? Have the youngsters take measurements and draw diagrams. How about studying the measurements of the Capitol Building in Washington—and other famous buildings? Learning becomes much more interesting if you use this approach. A triangle is not nearly as

Official Photograph—Board of Education, City of N.Y

Figure 6-4

interesting as a triangularly shaped building. A circle pales in comparison with a baseball park such as Shea Stadium.

Dramatization

Can you remember when you were a child? How would you have liked taking part in the game which follows? Most little boys and girls love it.

Make a large circle, with every child in the class taking his place in it. Then direct every third child to go into the center. (In a group of 30, this places ten—which is the number needed.) Each child sings the words, while those in the center act them out.

> Ten little boys on their way to school.
> Now there are nine—one jumped in the pool.
> Nine little boys out on a spree,
> But I see only eight—one's up a tree.
> Eight little boys looking up at heaven
> One ran away to hide—now there are seven.
> Seven little boys picking up sticks.
> One fell down—then there were six.
> Six little boys standing near a hive.
> One got stung—now there are five.
> Five little boys standing near the door.
> One ran out—then there were four.
> Four little boys sailing out to sea.
> One got seasick—now there are three.
> Three little boys heard a cow moo.
> One went to see it—then there were two.
> Two little boys out in the sun.
> One got sunburned—now there is one.
> One little boy when his work is done.
> He fell asleep—and now there is none.

Repeat this, making sure each child has one opportunity to be in the center.

This device teaches subtraction, but similar songs may be used for addition, as well.

The Mathematics of Trips

Many of your children may never take long trips, but calculating distances, rates of speed, acceleration, and velocity by using maps is far more exciting than reading a problem from a textbook. It is possible, too, to integrate learnings in geography, history, and mathematics by so doing. How far, for example, did Brigham Young and the Mormons travel before they reached the "right place"—the location today of Salt Lake City?

Using latitude and longitude figures to do calculations of distances is good arithmetic practice as well. Even young children can learn that the 360° of the circle are the basis for the lines of longitude. Calculating the distance from Greenwich, England to Bombay, or to New York, is of interest to them, and the results are often surprising to the children.

Take your class on imaginary trips. "We're leaving San Francisco today by car, bound for Mexico City. If we must get there in four days, how far would we have to go each day, if we want to cover approximately the same number of miles per day?"

How far is it from Maine's most northern tip to Florida's most southern? There is an endless amount of arithmetic to be tied in with map study—and it's fun!

Link the time zones to this, too. This gives your children exercises in logic as well as in calculations. We used a riddle: "How fast will a plane have to travel so that a person going from New York to Los Angeles will be there before he left?" This requires knowledge of time zones—and much thought—on the part of your children. (The answer is determined this way. There are four time zones in our country, representing three hours of time difference. It is three hours earlier in Los Angeles than New York. Therefore if a person left New York at noon, it would be 9 in Los Angeles, but 12 on his watch. If the trip took less than three hours, he would reach Los Angeles before 12—Los Angeles time. Of course, it would be nearing 3 P.M.—New York time— but before 12 in Los Angeles.

Have your classes work on problems of this nature—because of their interest, and because of the thought processes involved.

Calculating Food Production and Population Figures

This can involve decimals, percentages, maps, and graph study, as well as the fundamental skills. The seriousness of overpopulation can be brought out to the children, in addition to the work in arithmetic. You should work with statistics in regard to growth of plants, production of cattle, the catching of fish. Here we are using numbers to teach concepts, such as dealing with the problem of feeding the billions of people in the world. You may use this work as drills in the use of large numbers—hundreds of thousands, millions, even billions.

Mathematics of Biology

It is interesting to link arithmetic to biology. Some of the interesting problems you can present are:

- Calculate the amount of times the heart beats in a minute, day, hour.
- How far does the blood travel in a minute, day, or hour?
- Consider the width of capillaries, the number of white and red blood cells, and the fact that most capillaries can handle only one cell at a time—they are that narrow.

Using these examples, your children can be taught to use extremely small numbers. You can bring out the value of the microscope at the same time, and concepts of magnification.

Economics of Our Daily Lives

This is extremely important. Consider real jobs, by using advertisements from the newspapers. Then consider wages per hour, week, year; include overtime. Be sure to show how future earnings are related to education. Select advertisements for professionals, for skilled and for unskilled persons. Have them calculate the hourly, weekly, and yearly wages of each. Point out the return on four years of college, and on two years of college, in comparison with the return a high school graduate may expect.

On page 62 of Chapter 3, statistics are included which are very valuable for this topic. They give the figures for expected earnings for every level of education.

This work supplies material for using the fundamental skills and relating them to your pupils' lives.

Multiplication, division, percentages, decimals are all easily taught by the use of this topic. Children can be taught, too, the concept of the minimum wage—and how that influences the salary every worker earns.

You can link budgeting to this, as well. Budgets the children calculate, based on real salaries, are good. Also have the children budget their allowances—so that they understand "where their money goes."

Series of Suggestions

1. In teaching fractions, compare them with parts of a dollar. Be sure that you teach every child how to change bills into coins, how to handle money, and how to make change.

2. As soon as your children can master the concept of interest, explain this to them—so that they see the advantage of saving money in a bank which pays them interest. Point out that money on deposit for a long time will earn a great deal of interest, and if they save now, that money will be worth a great deal more as they grow older.

3. During the baseball season divide your class into groups, and assign a specific team to each group. Then, during the season, compare batting averages, games won–games lost, percentages, and make use of the large amount of calculating which is necessary to have your children work with figures.

4. Plan parties, picnics, and other school functions with the children, and have them calculate the costs, the percentages paid by each child.

5. Explain the Withholding Tax, the Social Security contributions, and even the various health plans to your children. Consider the differences as the income changes, and have them calculate this. If the children are interested, you may consider teaching them the graduated income tax, and having them determine the taxes of actors and actresses, and of millionaires.

6. Fifth graders are very often interested in horses. Problems related to them—the costs of food, care and lodging, and the odds on racing will often be greeted happily by the boys and girls.

7. Because we live during times where philanthropy is necessary, you might wish to use this problem to illustrate it. A little girl of our acquaintance, who is ten years old, earns $50 every year by making and selling fudge. She contributes 10 per cent of her earnings to buy toys for the children in a hospital in her neighborhood. At this rate, how much of her earnings will she have contributed to buy toys for these sick children when she reaches the age of 89? By bringing up the concept of helping others in an adroit manner, you are able to plant thoughts and ideas in the children's minds. It is to be desired that they grow and flourish.

8. Math riddles and puzzles are an excellent method of teaching children to think logically. For this reason, we suggest you be on the

lookout for them—and use them often. One classic goes, "A millionaire said to one of his servants, 'You may have anything you wish —for you have saved my life. Think about this, and make your decision. It should be reasonable, and if it is, I will grant it.' The servant replied, 'I am most reasonable, sir, and all I ask of you is this: Give me a penny the first day, and double it each day for one year.' The millionaire agreed immediately." Was he happy about his agreement at the end of the year? How much had it cost him?

9. Many of our young gentlemen are very interested in automobiles. A unit on costs—of cars, insurance, gasoline, and repairs will capture their interest—and, with a little guidance from the teacher, the girls' as well. You may discuss trading in cars and the amount of money lost in depreciation; the variation in insurance rates and how they are determined; gasoline mileage, and even the octane ratings are possibilities. Diagrams, graphs, and charts may be made relative to this topic. You will find children will be willing and anxious to do their homework when the topics are so relevant to their lives.

Personal Graphs

Have your children learn to make graphs, and pit them against themselves by giving a short quiz every week and having them graph the results. Each week have them place a point on the graph, and if the line goes up, give them a reward. (Of course it's impossible to go up from 100—so for those children, give them 5 points—start their graph at 95 so they "improve" even if they get 98 or 96.) You can have fun by changing the rewards; one week give candy kisses; another a foreign stamp; another a paper clip. Be sure your children realize this is a fun thing—not a serious reward. The point is to make their graphs go up, or hold at a top point.

This device can be used even with second graders. *But* make sure the children do not feel pressured.

Also give them material all week which will really prepare them for the quiz—so that they can do well.

Tell them in advance that they will be starting new graphs in September; immediately after Thanksgiving; after Washington's birthday; after Easter. In this way new starting points are established.

Grading Quizzes

Allow the children in your class to grade their own set of papers. Each time give the set to one child to do. Make sure he or she understands exactly what is expected. Also stress honesty, and the fact that you know the child wouldn't ever change a grade or do anything to alter anyone else's paper. Mark his, with him, showing him the correct answers. Do not give any part credit on these quizzes.

By having each child mark papers, you build the self-image of every member of the class. Even the slow children can handle the assignment, and they love to do it. It is obvious that this will save you a great deal of time, too.

Use ten or 20 examples, to make the marking simpler. Do not neglect to go over the results though, with the class—and to make any changes which might be necessary.

This system of marking gives children experiences in using numbers, and develops their feelings of self-worth.

Conclusion

In this chapter, we have suggested a number of methods with which you can make your teaching have an impact on the lives of your children. In science, we have worked with experiments involving natural phenomena, and with the construction of devices to illustrate scientific principles. Recommendations for growing plants, under a variety of conditions, are given. We have discussed eliminating superstitions and studying fascinating aspects of ourselves. We have included chemistry and food production, and a discussion of hobbies which originate in the study of science. We stress the need to educate our children—so that they are aware of the dangers of narcotics and the possible hazardous effects of smoking. We have, too, suggested many places to which you may take your classes—to make the world your classroom.

In arithmetic, we have included a strategy for competitive drills, so that they seem to be a game. By simulating stores, banks, and even stock exchanges, you can teach your children—while they are "playing." We hope you will have them measure and construct to learn measurements. There is a technique for dramatization which little ones will love, and they will also simultaneously learn to subtract. Children may also learn to calculate the costs of trips, and work with figures in regard to world food production. We have combined arithmetic with biology for some interesting ideas. The economics of our daily lives are very important, and should be taught again and again to our children—stressing the tremendously important aspect of earning a living, and some of the factors which affect it. Graphing should be done by the children, so that they may see their own progress, and they should be given the opportunity, too, to grade their own tests.

In science and in mathematics, as in all learning, the extent to which the work is directly related to the children's lives is the extent to which it will truly be successful. If we have opened your eyes to ways of determining this, of giving your children experiences rather than hypothetical cases, we have been successful. And your children will have benefited, and will benefit—tremendously.

··· 7 ···

Special Activities
for Social Studies and
Foreign Language Classes

~~~~~~~~~~~~~~~~~~~~~~~~~~~~~~~~~~~~~

EXPERIENCING SOCIAL STUDIES

We should consider two distinct areas in social studies. One is teaching our boys and girls to work harmoniously with one another, and the other is teaching the concepts and facts of geography, history, and current events. To these ends, we have suggested projects and committee work. A method is outlined for developing social consciousness in your youngsters. We discuss a "Viewpoint Free-for-All" or "Devil's Advocate Debate," which develops in your children the ability to see two sides to an issue, avoiding a one-track mindedness.

There is a technique presented which makes a study of the United Nations experiential by having children take the role of delegates to the United Nations. By interviewing the members of the older generations, your children are encouraged to learn from their experiences, and also to bridge the generation gap. A social studies newspaper is recommended, as is a "Travel Fair" and a social studies survey of your environment. Opinion polls, celebrity parties, the "If I lived there" method of teaching geography, folk music, and famous speeches are introduced. Trips are suggested and highly recommended. All of these techniques will enable you to make your teaching of social studies memorable, significant, and experiential.

The Socializing Aspect of Social Studies

The socializing aspect of social studies is more important than factual history and geography. For this reason, the methods we use to teach social studies should involve children working together—on projects, in committees, making parties, visiting shut-ins, or writing to pen pals. We must make our children feel for other human beings —and this cannot possibly be done by instructing them. We cannot teach getting along with other people unless we present opportunities which require our children to do so.

We, therefore, suggest you use committee work as often as possible.

Committees should consist of several children, or more—but no more than seven or eight, because the chances for real interaction will be cut down if the group is too large.

Research may be done by committees, and so may reporting. Even interpreting maps, drawing them, or making plaster of Paris reliefs is done well by a committee. Do not lose sight of the fact that children need to learn to work together, although much time is needed to teach this. It is probably much simpler and quicker to ask one child to make a map, but the other important aspect of social studies is thus ignored.

During these lessons, while children are working together, you may easily teach the need for, and the value of good manners—emphasizing the concept that good manners are naturally and spontaneously the expression of a kind heart. Remind your children always that the welfare of the group is the first consideration—whether it be a family, a classroom, or a committee. This will make for camaraderie, and automatically will help to eliminate discipline problems. As Shakespeare so sagely said, "A soft voice is an excellent thing in a woman," and we might add it is an asset for any human being. Incidentally, a child's personality is enhanced if his or her voice is soft and musical, rather than strident and raucous. The teacher, too, whose voice is controlled and trained, can be a fine example of this. It is far better to have the children strain their ears to hear what you have to say than shut them to ward off harsh sounds.

Social studies will be more effective if it is related to the lives of the children, and to the social needs of the day. Let us cite an important example of this aspect of teaching.

Some years ago, a shortage of food had arisen in an institution for the aged, located not far from the school in which one of the authors had been teaching. The principal asked her to make the rounds of the classrooms to obtain some cans of food to help alleviate this shortage. At the moment, the most important thought was to obtain an abundance of food—but as the project progressed, as the children warmed up to the idea and eagerly participated, with faces that beamed with genuine interest, bringing in far more food than had been anticipated

—she realized, with a thrill of pleasure, that she was teaching one of the most important lessons of her life. The children enjoyed bringing the food to school, and as they saw the walls being covered with the cans, their eyes shone with pride. The children learned more from this than from any textbook they or she could have read.

A charming representative from the Home for the Aged came to say "thank you." The principal estimated that one out of every three children had contributed food. Others brought in boxes and ropes to pack it. It was evident that this was, indeed, a "labor of love."

Make no mistake! This was a real, live, joyous lesson in social studies—not one which was dull and flat and stale.

The opportunities for social involvement are many. Be on the alert —then use them with alacrity. We promise you that they will bring satisfaction to your children's hearts and to you. Any time there is an emergency anywhere in the world, the Red Cross, the Salvation Army, and many, many other organizations will be happy to have you and your children participate with them in the alleviation of human misery. The children will be living their lessons as well as learning them.

The Viewpoint Free-for-All or Devil's Advocate Debate

Do you want to have a particularly stimulating lesson, perhaps for visiting parents or supervisors, or hopefully for your children themselves? The following technique is absolutely marvelous for this purpose.

Whenever you have studied a situation in which there have been two or more different points of view, set up a Viewpoint Free-for-All. This is structured in this way: Choose one child to moderate the discussion and recognize speakers from the floor. Then have two or three children represent each side. But, and this is most important, be sure these children realize they must try to think in the manner in which the people involved would think, and, when necessary, play the "devil's advocate." For example, we saw such a debate on "Eighteen years old—old enough to go to war, old enough to vote." Most, if not all, of the children believed 18-year-olds should vote, but, because we had some taking the opposing view, and arguing it with all their hearts, the debate and discussion were fabulous. Another possible topic is "A Woman for President of the United States." Here it will be easier to find children taking opposing viewpoints.

Many issues of current events may be handled effectively in this manner, as may events in the history of the nation and the world. Encourage the children to do research to back up their points of view.

By using this technique, we help our children to see more than one side of a given situation, and prevent them from developing "one-track minds." They are being trained to be broad, rather than narrow in their thinking, and to weigh and consider other viewpoints, whether they agree with them or not. This will make for socialization, and for wholesome discipline, which we hope will be carried out of the classroom into the homes, and hopefully, into the lives of our children.

Experientially Teaching About the United Nations

In studying the United Nations, have your children represent the countries in the Security Council, and give them an issue to discuss. For preparation, have them listen to the Security Council on radio, on tape, or see a film of it. Without doubt the best possible preparation would be to take them on a trip to the United Nations, in New York City, and if at all possible, see and hear an actual meeting. Try to encourage the children to really identify with the land they are representing.

Choose the issue for the debate carefully, from past history, or from the events of the day. Be sure that the children in your class have done research, and have been taught both the procedures for the discussion and the facts they need for it. For example, they would elect a President of the General Assembly before they started any discussion.

The same general procedure may be used with the General Assembly and for the Security Council—each child in the class representing one nation.

You may have the children draw flags, and have the flags hung at the front of the room—in the manner the flags are flown in front of the U.N. building in New York City.

You may give your children the opportunity to see how much time is spent in debate and discussion in the attempts by the United Nations to bring about a better world.

The children should be encouraged to bring in worthwhile clippings from newspapers and magazines regarding the United Nations, and a class scrapbook made for reference use and display. Photographs, graphs, and other material will heighten the interest of this collection.

In language arts, you may wish to include composition work on such subjects as "How Can We, as Individuals, Aid in the Work of the United Nations?" In art, posters can be made with this theme in mind. You may wish to send this work, the compositions, and the posters to the United Nations, which often publishes material of this kind.

Interviewing "Old Timers"

Years ago families lived together—grandparents, parents, children, aunts, uncles, cousins. Today this is no longer true, and there is far too little interchange of ideas between the generations. We believe

Figure 7-1

there should be such an interchange because the children can learn a great deal from it, and because it will serve as a means of bridging the generation gap. One of the areas in which older folk can contribute is by tales of "the old country," or by stories of the days when the automobile was so young people used to shout, "Get a horse."

Have your children interview their grandparents or other senior citizens, asking such specific questions as the following:

> "In what ways was your life different from mine when you were my age?"
> "Why did you leave the country (city, town) where you were born?"
> "Do you believe this country is really a melting pot? Why?"
> "Do you believe it is really the land of opportunity? Why?"
> "Do you think your life would have been better or worse if you had stayed? Why?"

Have each child report and discuss his findings with the class.

Social Studies Newspaper

Results of the interviews above, or of various research projects, may be incorporated into a social studies newspaper or magazine. Illustrations, poems, humorous articles, and cartoons may be contributed.

One use for these newspapers is with the class producing them. Another is with classes coming after, who love to look at work of previous classes. It inspires them, and gives them ideas which serve as a basis for their newspaper. Such an endeavor should be duplicated and distributed. Try to get a contribution from every child.

Travel Fair

Set up many "travel agencies" in your class. Assign two to three children per agency, representing one country, and have them construct simple booths, decorating them with their own posters. Have them research the country, so they can answer questions, and interview persons who have visited it. Show souvenirs, dolls, etc. They may write to the Consulate or Embassy for material, or may consult magazines for photographs and articles.

When you hold your Fair, have one child man the booth, while the others visit their classmates. Alternate so each child sees every booth, and also runs his own for a time. This may be worked in with foreign language study as well, if you wish.

Exploring Your Immediate Environment

Many people are abysmally ignorant of their immediate environment. A very worthwhile research project is one which has the children:

1. Find the number, location, and description of all schools (public, parochial, or private; elementary, junior or senior high, or college; vocational or trade).
2. The parks—their specific locations and facilities available.
3. Businesses or factories employing many people and description of each.
4. Libraries.
5. Theatres.
6. Historic sites or places of unusual interest.
7. Bridges and tunnels, the bodies of water they are needed to cover, and the places they connect.
8. A brief history of the area—who settled it, where they came from, how they earned a living.

Use a project of this kind to build pride in the community. Find things for your boys and girls to be proud of and build on these. This will help your children develop feelings of self-worth, which are so important.

Opinion Polls

People are interested in what other people think, as may be seen by the success of Messrs. Gallup and Harris. When there is an issue of import, with a divergence of public opinion, assign polling to your children. Work with them on the preparation of the specific items for which they are seeking information. For example, "Do you think an atomic power plant should be built on the banks of the _____ River?"

"Why did you vote as you did?"

"How do you think this will affect the community?"

Official Photograph—Board of Education, City of N.Y

Figure 7-2

In an election year, you may have the class take a "straw poll." Be sure to include a discussion of the method used for getting a fair sampling of the population being polled.

Celebrity Parties Are Fun—and Educational, Too

Give each child the name of a historical character he will represent. Have him research this person thoroughly. Then have each child represent this individual at the party. The members of the class have to guess who it is by questioning. They are to keep lists, and see who guesses the most. The questions would be similar to those asked while playing 20 questions—but, of necessity, they have to work very quickly. Use a party situation—soda and candy will ac-

150

complish this—and the lesson is very well motivated because it is truly a "party."

Geography

"If I lived there" is the assignment you give. Have your children find out, "Where would I live?" "What would I eat?" "What would I wear?" "What would my life be like?" "Would I go to school?" "How would my parents earn a living?" "What is life like—in cities and on farms?" "What would my life expectancy be?" Personalize the lessons by putting the child into the country.

Stamps, coins, and foods may be exhibited. Charts may be made showing the language of the land.

This may be combined with the Travel Fair mentioned previously.

Comparing Different Things

Comparison of various items make interesting exhibits and dioramas or charts, and you may wish to have committees work on these. Ships, other forms of transportation, means of communication, houses, farming implements, rockets are but a few of the items which may be studied.

Folk Music

The folk music of a nation often gives a picture of that country, and children will enjoy hearing, singing, and playing such music. As an example, we cite "The Banana Boat Song," sung by Jamaican workers as they load the boats. There are a huge number of such songs, which give a picture of some aspect of life in their land of origin.

Famous Speeches

Possibly the most famous speech ever made was given by Abraham Lincoln, "Fourscore and seven years ago . . ." There are many famous speeches and hearing them builds a closeness between orator, though often dead, and the child. Have your children read the speeches, and when they fully understand them, read them aloud or even recite them to their classmates. Choose speeches, however, which

Photo courtesy Dept. of the Interior, Natl. Park Service, Edison Natl. Historic Site

Figure 7-3. The library of Thomas A. Edison which contains over 10,000 books, Edison's desk, his cot, and many other items of interest (Edison National Historic Site, West Orange, N. J.).

have impact, and which will enrich the child. For example, use Franklin D. Roosevelt's "We have nothing to fear but fear itself."

Please Take Your Children on Trips!

A most vital and important part of the effective teaching of social studies is taking your pupils on trips. Watch with what anticipation even a short trip is greeted! It is a break in the humdrum, a change from routine, and truly a learning experience.

Canvas the resources your community has to offer. List them, and then discuss the proposed trips with the class—allowing them to make the final decision.

Each child should at some time see the places of historic interest —the national historic sites, such as the Edison National Historic Site, West Orange, N.J., and monuments in the area. They build a sense of continuity with the past. Many cities have a number of such places within the immediate area. Besides these, consider the following:

- Any large industrial plant or factory, which offers tours.
- The office of your local newspaper.
- Airports.
- Piers or docks.
- Game preserves or wildlife refuges.

Consider, too, trips outside of your immediate area. Surely a trip to Washington, D.C., New York, Chicago, Detroit, or Los Angeles is worthwhile. Your children should visit the capital of their state as well.

We believe, that as transportation costs decrease, school trips to Europe and the Orient will be taken as the entire world becomes your classroom.

Traveling is a series of vital, important experiences, and, as teachers, we should try to bring as many such experiences to our youngsters as possible.

Studying whaling? Mystic Seaport in Connecticut, literally puts you in a whaling town, and even on board a ship. Life in the colonies —start in Jamestown, and then move on to Williamsburg, Virginia. There are a countless number of places worthwhile visiting.

Trips, far and near, add spice to life and to learning. Three or four during the school year are not too many.

Audio-Visual Aids

The times we live in are most assuredly different from those in which most of us grew up, and with these changing times have come new variations on old devices, enabling us to offer many new experiences through the use of audio-visual aids. Surely you are familiar with most of them: the chalkboard, which we used to call the black-

Official Photograph, Colonial Williamsburg, Williamsburg, Virginia

Figure 7-4. Once the seat of government of a vast and powerful Virginia colony that stretched to the Mississippi, the colonial Capitol building at Williamsburg has been carefully reconstructed to the appearance of the early 1700's. Here met the House of Burgesses, America's first representative legislative assembly. Also, it was in the eighteenth-century Capitol in Williamsburg that Patrick Henry gave his famous speech against the Stamp Act.

board (and in most schools is no longer black, but green, to prevent eyestrain), the charts, drawings, cartoons, and even reproductions of famous paintings, are all effective for use in social studies, as well

Official Photograph, Colonial Williamsburg, Williamsburg, Virginia

Figure 7-5. The George Wythe House–This handsome brick house, home of a distinguished scholar-statesman, is one of the original structures in Williamsburg, Virginia, restored to its eighteenth-century appearance. George Wythe, first law professor in America and a signer of the Declaration of Independence, was the mentor of Thomas Jefferson.

as in other subjects. There are many new aids, however, which are more sophisticated.

1. *Films.* These are often obtainable, easily, from commercial companies for a small fee, or even gratis. Your school library may have a book listing these.

2. *Filmstrips.* They are an invaluable aid. Easily shown, with a simple machine, in a relatively short time, and presenting information and pictures in a painless manner, the children enjoy them—and learn from them. They are stored in a small space, and a library may be built at moderate cost. To effectively use the filmstrip, be sure you preview it first. If the boys and girls need practice in oral reading, you may have them read the captions aloud. If not, have them read them silently, and then ask them questions about the material they read. By adroit questioning, you can teach the youngsters to read for content and ideas. You may choose to give the class a list of four or five questions before viewing, which they are to answer from information they gain viewing the filmstrip.

3. *The Overhead Projector.* This device has a great many applications. Using a blank transparency, you are able to write directly upon it, instead of writing on the board. This enables you to keep your eyes on the children at all times, which is a most effective measure when dealing with restless children.

You may use the overhead projector to project solid objects, such as beads to represent chromosomes. You may show photographs, as well, if they are positives instead of prints. Maps with overlays are particularly useful in social studies. You might show the United States as it is today; place an overlay on the map, and the original 13 colonies are delineated. Remove the overlay, replace it with a second one, outlining the addition of Florida or the Louisiana Purchase. Used this way, the projector fascinates children. Diagrams drawn on blank transparencies are more arresting, more compelling to look at than if they are in a textbook. Cartoons are marvelous, and comic strip characters very good.

Allow your children to place the materials on the stage of the projector. The procedure is an extremely easy one, and they will enjoy the experience. Also permit them to write on the blank transparency. This machine is truly an aid to the teacher.

4. *Kinescopes.* Kinescopes are really moving pictures with sound. They are the films used to telecast various productions, and they are frequently available on a rental basis. The many fine programs we see can subsequently be used for teaching purposes. We suggest you arrange for rental with a group of teachers. The best of television

becomes available when and where you want it. The commercials have been removed—but, even if they are not, the children seem to enjoy seeing them, for the simple reason they realize they do not belong in school. The kinescopes do, though; try them, and see how your children react.

5. *Tape Recorders.* Tapes are available of many radio broadcasts, and are easily obtained, gratis, or at low cost. The tape recorder, though, is best used to record your children's voices, and replay them. Make recordings of debates, discussions, or reports early in the year, and then replay them later. The children enjoy this thoroughly, and you can compare their earlier responses with those they would make now.

6. *Television.* Surely television may be considered an audio-visual aid. We have discussed this medium in Chapter 5, devoted to the language arts. However, it is just as pertinent to the study of the social sciences. We suggest you utilize it in the same way we recommended in the English curriculum.

FUN IN FOREIGN LANGUAGE CLASSES

Basic to all successful teaching is the desire to make learning a pleasurable experience. This may prove to be a bit difficult for teachers of many subjects, but not for those whose area is foreign language. Surely the classes must become more than groups of children who are parroting the teacher. Our aims should be threefold; we must give the children a familiarity with the language, and a facility with it, so that they not only speak it, but also are capable of thinking in it. We should also give the children a knowledge of all the countries wherein the language is spoken. Spanish, for example, obviously originated in Spain, but there are a large number of nations where it is the official tongue. Most of all, the mastery of the language should offer to all children a feeling of satisfaction. We want them to get pleasure from their ability to communicate in a tongue other than their own native one. We hope to do these things, and, at the same time, structure the situation so that the children will have fun; it is with these objectives in mind that we suggest the following methods and strategies.

Structuring the Situation So That Our Children Speak, Really Speak, the Language

As we learned our native tongue by constant repetition, so we must teach foreign languages. This is best done by speaking as little English as possible to the children during their foreign language class time. Each day greet the class with the customary greeting. "Bon jour," or "Buenos días," you say. Expect the response in like manner. If you wish them to reply in unison, you might say, "Buenos días, clase." (Good day, class.) Then ask individual children, "How are you?" Equip them to answer with such expressions as "So, so," or "Fine, thanks." Next use the drill which follows: it is all spoken in the foreign language:

"Today is ...., the .... of ...."

(Today is Monday, the fourth of January, 1969, for example.)

Have several youngsters repeat this, particularly at the beginning of the term.

"It is .... in the morning." (It is nine o'clock in the morning.)

"The sun is shining today." (Or any sort of short weather report. For example, one might say, "It is cold and clear." Or, "It is cold and it seems likely we may have snow.")

By repeating this drill daily, your children gain facility and use the words they will often need in ordinary conversation. Next announce, "Our work for today is ...." and proceed with the lesson.

This type of repetition is valid because it is not forced or artificial. Indeed, these are conversations we hold daily. It is excellent for the slow learner, who will be able to master much of the material taught because of the repetition. It also enables the children to reply intelligently when they are asked, "And what foreign language are you studying? Oh, French—comment allez vous?"

Have the children call you "Señor, señorita, señora," or "Monsieur, herr" (as the case may be), all of the time. This type of association helps to get them to think in the language. Call the boys and girls by the foreign equivalent of their names. Joseph becomes José, Mary is María, Henry is Enrique, and Paul is Pablo.

If you wish to enlarge the warm-up conversation, you may ask about the children's families, about school happenings, or you may wish to discuss a current event—all in the foreign language, of course. Be sure, though, that the subjects are not artificial or uninteresting. Make these conversations similar to those you have with friends.

Teach Songs in the Foreign Language

Beginning on the first day of class, teach your children songs in the foreign language. A child will learn "La Plume de ma Tante" much more quickly than he would a series of vocabulary words. Do not limit your teaching of songs to the very elementary ones. "Frere Jacques" is fine for one of the initial selections, but as your class progresses, move on to more complex songs. "El Rancho Grande," "Allouette," "Amapola," or "Die Gedenken Sind Frei"—the list is truly endless. If you have ever studied French, we are sure you remember, "Allons, Enfants de la Patrie." You may use recordings to augment your work, and if there are any children in the class who can play, or even strum guitars, invite them to bring the instruments to school to accompany the songs. You, and the children, too, will enjoy this kind of teaching. Be relaxed in regard to the singing, for if you are not, if you become grim, all the fun goes out of the music. Make sure all of the children are able to translate the songs, if not verbatim, at least for general meaning. This is an ingenious way to almost "sneak in" vocabulary.

It is fun, too, to translate songs freely from English into the foreign language. You may do this yourself, or assign it to the children. It is not necessary to hold to the literal translation of the words. A free translation is more interesting, more stimulating, and far more easily achieved. Experiment with the technique, because it adds much vitality to the class. Allow children to sing the translation. Another method, rather similar, is to utilize a familiar song, and have the class write additional words or parodies to it—in the foreign language. Television commercials, for example, sound very amusing when translated, and parodying them is quite entertaining.

Be sure to give the boys and girls the lyrics to any songs you expect them to learn. They may copy them, or you may distribute rexographed copies, but in either case you will find you help them immensely.

Play "Simon Says" in Your Foreign Language

"Simon dit, Simon dit, — — — — —"
Your children will love, and respond well to this game. Teach the

159

commands first and then have fun! The leader gives the commands to the children, who are standing in rows in front of him. If he says "Simon dice — — — — —," they must obey. If he gives the command without the "Simon says," they must not do what was instructed. If they do perform the action, they are out of the game, and must leave it.

As the term progresses, make the commands more involved. If you inject humor—scratch your nose, rub your stomach, flap your arms like wings and fly, your children will have a wonderful time. We suggest you take the role of Simon the first few times, until the children have learned the commands; then you may have one of the boys or girls, who is fluent in the language, take charge. Set up the rules before the games start, and be sure they are obeyed by having the children enforce them. Use "Simon says" every three or four weeks. If played more often, it will lose its appeal. Make sure that your slow learners have mastered the vocabulary necessary, so that they may participate and enjoy themselves.

Take Your Children to See Films in the Foreign Language

There are many foreign films available. (We cannot stress too strongly that you, personally, preview the film first, making sure it is suitable for the children, and can be considered to be part of the curriculum.) If you can find films which do not have titles, these are better, because your aim in having the children see the film is to have the boys and girls hear the language spoken in a life situation. When you plan this type of trip, give a specific assignment; it may be a series of simple questions that the children are to answer, a short paragraph that they are to write, or a short talk they are to prepare.

If there is no theatre in your immediate area which exhibits movies of this type, perhaps you can rent a film and show it. Invite the parents of your children—either to take part in the trip or view the showing. Seeing "Don Quixote," "The Two of Us," or even "My Fair Lady" performed in a foreign language will bring enjoyment and help your children absorb the language, and develop a feeling for it. Explain to them that they will not understand every word, but they will hear expressions they can comprehend, and are to try to get the gist of the story.

Eating in a Foreign Language

Do a unit on foods—teaching the names of the various foods in your language. You may wish to decorate your room by displaying posters, using pictures from magazines—with the appropriate words. The children may also design menus, find recipes, or make scrapbooks using terms in the foreign language. Then, as the culmination of this unit, you may choose any or all of the following methods:

- Plan a trip, with the entire class, to a foreign restaurant, and encourage the children to order from the menu. It is suggested that you visit the restaurant first, to be sure the food is good, and is not too expensive. Be sure "hamburger" is on the menu—because, for many young people, it is their staff of life.
- Should you prefer, you might consult with the children and their parents, and decide to prepare a class dinner, consisting

Official Photograph—Board of Education, City of N.Y

Figure 7-6

161

of foreign foods. You may limit the food to that of your "mother country" or you may make it a "dinner of all nations." In either event, select a committee to correlate the dishes, so that the items brought in are varied—children or parents can combine talents in one or two main dishes, or you may be able to offer an even larger variety.

Popular Records of the Mother Country

Young people love records. They need to hear the foreign tongue spoken as much as possible, and combining these two ideas, we are able to utilize recordings to lighten and brighten our teaching. Have the children look for such records. Even American songs, translated, have value. This technique is worth trying because it motivates, and brings into the children's sphere the contributions of musicians and groups singing in other languages.

Pen Pals

"Querida Lisa," (the letter read).

"Me llamo Aida y vivo en Mexico, D.F. Tengo un hermano y dos hermanas."

With what excitement the letter from Aida was greeted. "I wonder how old she is?" "She sounds nice." "What do you think she looks like?" All of the questions stemmed from a short note, but that short note gave the teacher the idea that pen pals, writing in foreign languages, might be an unusual experience. It surely proved to be.

Writing to children of approximately the same age has practical value for both participants. Should you decide to experiment with this, when you establish the exchange of letters, suggest to the children that they share the responses with their classmates. You may wish to help the children write their letters, by listing possible topics for them to include, giving them the vocabulary they need, and teaching them the idioms they will want to use. Letters may be written entirely in the foreign language, or as we prefer, "half and half." This gives each writer a chance to write frequently and to write in both his native tongue and in the foreign language he is studying. In some schools, teachers have arranged to have an entire class write to another class. Individual letters are written, but, to save postage, they are mailed together. We find the individual letter, mailed separately, is more meaningful, although it is more expensive.

Acculturation

When a child is studying Spanish, don't you think he should know some of the culture, history, and customs of the Spanish people? Don't we associate mantillas, Isabella, Hemingway, and fine suede with España? The Eiffel Tower, the tricolor, the Seine, and Coco Chanel with la belle France? Shouldn't we give our children similar associations? Costumes are not worn today, except in remote towns and villages, but they were until recently. Pictures of them add color and interest to your classroom. The artists in your class may draw posters illustrating them, which will beautifully decorate your room.

You may wish to have committees do projects on various cities— Florence or Rome, Toledo or Granada, Marseilles or Cannes. Have the children do research, as if they were planning a visit to the city, and wanted to become familiar with all of the places of interest. Then have them give oral reports. If they are able to obtain pictures, suggest they include them. (Old copies of the *National Geographic Magazine* are excellent for this purpose.)

Word Games

How many words can you find in Montmartre? Similar to the word game we play in English, this is fun in any language. For an interesting switch, allow either French or English words (assuming you are teaching French). Have the children write the word at the top of a sheet of paper, and list the words they can think of. Two points are awarded for each word in French, one for each in English. Offer small prizes, from the school supply room or the local dime store— pens, pencils, rulers. We feel that you award a prize because this is a game, although you are also reviewing vocabulary and motivating the lesson as well.

"Let's Tape That!"

When there is some activity taking place in your class which will prove intriguing when taped, by all means use this device. Children are enamoured of gadgets and using the tape recorder is fun—great fun. They may be permitted to tape speeches, playlets, songs, or reports, and will be delighted to hear them played back. We suggest you retain the tapes and play them again at the end of the term. This is guaranteed to please your children.

You may wish to "make a recording" of the entire class singing "Songs of Sunny Spain," or "Under Blue Parisian Skies," or you may wish to use several soloists with guitar accompaniment. Above all, be tasteful in the selection of the songs and the music, and seek perfection in the pronunciation of the language.

Signs

Decorate your classroom with signs in the foreign language—so that your children, when their gaze is caught, are almost forced to think in that language. Have your boys and girls make these signs, translating such things as proverbs, witticisms, comments about life, advertisements, and comical remarks. For example, you may have a saying such as Mark Twain's "The weather—everyone talks about it, but no one does anything about it." Or "People who live in glass houses should pull down their window shades."

Cartoons are attractive and attention getting. Utilize the talents of any children in your classes, requesting they make these to be displayed in the classroom.

Playlets

Divide your class into groups and have each group produce a playlet—in the language they are studying. Furnish the children with words they might require, and then teach them to the entire class, so that they will understand the playlet when it is produced. Groups may write their own plays or translate scenes from famous plays.

You may wish to assign these before national holidays, such as Valentine's Day or Christmas. When possible, encourage the children to be humorous in their selection of material, and to be dramatic in their presentation. Music may surely be included. By using several groups, every child is drawn into the productions, which should be set up to guarantee each child a role. This is more difficult if only one or two playlets are produced.

Choose one child in each group to be the director. If there is a child who speaks the foreign language fluently, use his fluency by having him serve as the announcer or producer. If the playlets are particularly successful, you may wish to invite the parents to see them. If you do so, offer a written translation of the playlet, so that the adults can follow the dialogue.

Vocabulary Bees

Hold vocabulary bees, in the same manner as the old-fashioned spelling bee. Divide your class into teams, and have one child play the part of master of ceremonies, giving the words in the foreign language and having the children translate them into English. Then, after each child has been given one opportunity, have the English word given, and have the children give the translation into the foreign language. In this way, the slow learners are given the chance to participate. Then, as the bee progresses, the tasks become more difficult. Keep alternating until each team has one child left. Then give each a token prize. This eliminates hard feelings which sometimes occur in games of this nature.

Foreign Language Picture Dictionaries

To teach the children the names of familiar objects, you may have them make signs and attach them to such things as doors, windows, desks, chairs, and the like. This fixes the word to the object in the child's mind, and will facilitate the child's thinking of it in the foreign language. You may have the children draw diagrams of their houses, labeling each room with the items usually found in it.

To make a foreign language picture dictionary, allow the children to choose which type of pictures they wish to use—stick figures, drawings, paintings, or photographs cut from magazines. They may even

165

use combinations of all of these. Each is placed on a page, with the word describing it printed below. This type of book, alphabetically arranged, is a reference which the youngsters write themselves, and to which they can refer when necessary. They will enjoy making it, too, particularly if you encourage humor and creativity. Display the books when completed.

Translations

Train your children to try to translate printed words when they read them. For example, signs, advertisements, names of books and magazines, even the names of moving pictures, may all be translated, and by so doing, the children are helped to think in the foreign language.

Let's Take a Trip

Unfortunately, this is an imaginary trip—but it can be made fascinating. Have the children select a place they would like to visit. List the regions of the mother country, assigning one group to each region; for example, a French class might consider the Alps region, the Basque country, the Pyrenees, Brittany, Burgundy, Champagne, Alsace Lorraine, the Ile-de-France, the Loire Valley, Normandy, the Riviera, and Corsica. Each group might obtain travel posters, probably from travel agencies. (Suggest one child communicate with Trans-World Airlines. This very generous firm will send printed information, and possibly a speaker and a film.) The children should work out itineraries, learning about the places of interest within each region. They may write to the consulates or embassies for more information. You may wish to find a child whose parents have visited the place, and might enjoy showing films or slides of it. It is possible that no one has traveled to that area—in which case, perhaps there are filmstrips or moving pictures of the section available. The children may make drawings of some of the well-known places within their area, specifically what items it is famous for. For example, the Burgundy region is famous for its wines, and the Riviera for its bikinis. Records or tape recordings might be used to supply background music, and if the land being studied has sidewalk cafes, why not set one up in a corner of the classroom? Maps of the land, souvenirs, trinkets, and guidebooks would help reinforce the idea of taking a trip. Encourage the children to make this exciting. Do everything you can to bring a spirit of adventure to the lessons. Start as the plane leaves the airport and finish each trip as it returns home.

Using the Art of the Nation

The contributions of a nation's artists are among its most important riches. We can use the paintings, drawings, and sculpture in our teaching; for instance, France has the Impressionists, Spain El Greco and Goya, and Picasso today. When you bring this material to your children, you are introducing them to the greatest artists of all time. Who might better transport your boys and girls to Paris than Maurice Utrillo? How can a child be taught Italian without seeing a picture or replica of Michelangelo's "David"? You might describe these masterpieces, but pictures of them around the room are far more effective. By helping to develop their interest in art, you are broadening their horizons. To stimulate further interest, a trip to a museum of art may be arranged, which will introduce many of the youngsters to art treasures they never dreamed of. This is experiential learning at its best.

Newspapers and Magazines—in the Foreign Language

There are many shops which sell foreign language newspapers and magazines; these make fascinating teaching tools for the more advanced students. However, even your beginners will enjoy looking at them, and trying to figure out the gist of each article. You may wish to post some of the magazine covers, or the front pages of the newspapers, on the bulletin boards in your room to attract the children's attention.

Class Compositions in the Foreign Language

Writing class compositions is a fine activity to use when you are anxious to involve every child. Offer to the class a variety of subjects, and have the children select one. Then have each child prepare a sentence and submit it to you. Try to incorporate these into a composition. Very often the results can be clever or amusing. Topics such as the adventures of a cat or dog, a boy or girl are good. The subject

Official Photograph—Board of Education, City of N.Y

Figure 7-7

of the composition might be running away from home and going to Madrid or Paris. What adventures are encountered? Have foreign language dictionaries available for the children to consult. If the composition is worthwhile, have it rexographed and distribute a copy to each child. Use it for teaching reading in the foreign language in the same manner you might use an experience chart as reading material.

Making Your Foreign Language a Family Affair

Suggest to your children that they teach their families a word or phrase each evening at dinner. In the beginning it is wise for you to suggest specific material for use that evening, until the idea catches on. For example, the first day have the children teach the common greeting—Bon jour, buenos días, gutten tag, chiao. Then, "How are you?" Follow this with a suitable reply. Next, "Today is Monday," etc. The same rules should apply to conversation that have already been outlined—namely that it be real, rather than artificial, natural rather than contrived.

The children might explain to their parents that they are helping one another. The parents will enjoy helping their son or daughter, and they will be learning a little of the language at the same time. The children might wish to invite their parents to the foreign language class, and if you are willing to have them visit, it is an excellent means of gaining parental goodwill.

This is an activity which is of great value. It gives the child practice in speaking the language, and it gives him prestige at home. It may also be a pleasant way for the family to enjoy one another's company. If you suggest this activity to your classes, inquire about its progress from time to time. If you forget about it, so will the children; whereas, if you are interested, they will tell you of their experiences as "teachers."

Parlez-Vous Francais?

Encourage your children to speak the language to their friends, their classmates, their families. They can do this on their way to school, in the lunchroom, on the way home, and even on the telephone. Have them try to use words they have just learned, as well as those with which they are familiar. This will help them develop fluency, and will give each child added confidence in his ability.

On your part, teach the children the expressions they will need for this kind of conversation, by making sure that a large part of the vocabulary list is composed of words and phrases of a very practical nature. As soon as you can, inject humorous expressions, so that the conversation need not be dull. Encourage the use of gestures, and facial expressions, as well. Mais oui!!

Meet Cantinflas

Cantinflas is an enchanting Mexican gentleman, whom you may remember having seen in "Eighty Days Around the World." Shouldn't your students of Spanish know who he is? You may wish to obtain photographs of the movie and recording stars speaking your foreign language, and post them in your room. The boys and girls enjoy singing groups, and they may wish to contribute photographs of those singing in the foreign language. Other famous persons, too, in politics, in government, in the arts, and in history should be noted, and if possible, pictured. Try to bring your children as close as you can to people living in the country in which your foreign language is spoken.

Publishing a Foreign Language Magazine

Children are often capable of writing material which is worthy of publication, and you may use this as a motivational factor. We suggest you announce this idea, and have the children write themes, limericks, humorous anecdotes, draw pictures, and prepare puzzles —all in the foreign language. If the work the children do is of sufficient value, you and the other foreign language teachers may decide to have a school foreign language publication. You may also include the work on trips and the reports mentioned earlier in this chapter.

By skillful planning and decorating, this magazine may be made interesting and of value to you as a teaching tool; the children will take it home, read it, and enjoy it with their families.

Poster Fun

1. ¿Que Hora Es? Have each child draw and decorate a series of six clocks, making them as unusual and amusing as possible. Then have them indicate the time on the clock, and in words below it.

Instruct each child to draw one clock with hands on the hour, at ten minutes after the hour, at a quarter past, at half past, at a quarter to, and at ten to the next hour.

Suggest they make their clocks with peoples' faces or with animals, with stars or other objects—but make them as clever and as different as possible from a regular clock.

Use these posters to decorate your room. When they have been up for about a month, or even three weeks, replace them with other posters.

2. *My Day*. Have the children draw posters showing their daily activities—labeled in the foreign language. For example, have the children conjugate each verb—by having one child do a poster which says, "I get up, I get dressed, I have breakfast, I feed my dog, I go to school." Another child would draw and label a poster with "You get up, you get dressed, you have breakfast, you feed your dog, you go to school." Still another would draw "He gets up," etc. After these posters are made, use them to decorate your room, so that the children see these words again and again, in addition to hearing them.

The drawings may be stick figures, or regular figures, depending on the child's skill as an artist, or they may be cut out of magazines. Encourage ingenuity, so that the children's attention will be enticed by the posters.

Conclusion

All effective teaching affects the lives of our children. It falls into the realm of social studies to teach our boys and girls some of the really important concepts of life—such as cooperatively living and working together, through committees and projects, and helping one's fellowman.

To make social studies experiential, we have suggested a number of techniques—such as the "Devil's Advocate Debate" and the United Nations Student Delegate Assembly, which puts your pupils into actual situations through role-playing.

Using an interview technique, we introduce a method for learning of the experiences of older members of society.

Creating a social studies newspaper offers opportunities for cooperative work, as does a Travel Fair. Having your children do a survey of resources within the immediate environment helps them to develop pride in their community.

171

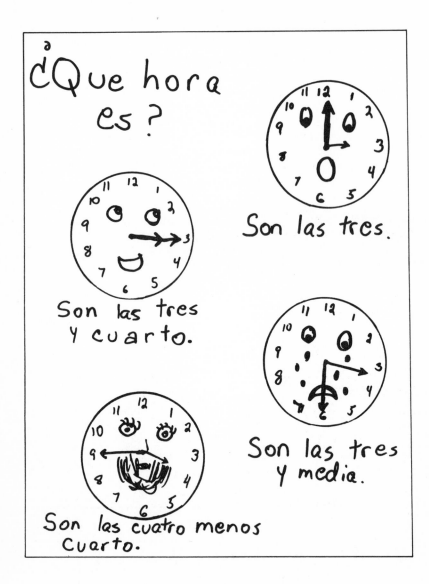

Figure 7-8

172

Opinion polls make current events come to life, and celebrity parties "bring back" famous persons in history. "If I lived there," is a method for teaching geography which makes it personal for each child, as does the use of folk music. Famous speeches are suggested to bring back the voices of the past. Trips are emphasized as a means of revitalizing your teaching, as are audio-visual aids. All of these techniques will, we hope, make your boys and girls love learning, and social studies.

Also, in this chapter, methods are listed to make the study of a foreign language, regardless of which it is, a series of interesting, entertaining, and rewarding experiences. We have chosen these techniques because they will help the students

Official Photograph—Board of Education, City of N.Y

Figure 7-9. Students at William J. Gaynor Junior High School showing mock-battle soldiers to Professor Edmund Morgan, Yale historian.

build a familiarity with the language, become more facile in speaking it, and we have included strategies, too, which will acquaint the children with the land of origin of the language they are studying—its people, customs, history, and geography. We have tried to involve the parents in our foreign language program in a manner which they will enjoy. But above all, we have tried to provide methods which will make this foreign language study a successful learning experience.

It is suggested that you structure your class so that your children will speak the language as much as possible, while in class, in and around the school, and even at home with their families and friends. We have stressed natural, normal conversation, and tried to show you how to foster it. Singing,

JUNTOS

Todos los pajaros trabajan y juegan juntos,
Todos los insectos trabajan y juegan juntos,
Todos los pescados trabajan y juegan juntos,
Por que nosotros, no?

Detra Sears
8-301

TOGETHERNESS

All birds work and play together,
All insects work and play together,
All fish work and play together,
Why can't we?

Translation by the author

From "Prall on Parade," Anning S. Prall Jr. H. S. Yearbook, Staten Island, N.Y.

Figure 7-10

LA LECON FRANCAISE

"Bonjour" is what you say
To someone when you see him coming your way.
In English it means good morning to you,
And I hope you have a pleasant day.
When you want to count to twenty,
You go from "un a vingt",
And instead of saying the dog,
Now you say "un chien".
The students are "eleves",
Who sit at "le pupitre"
And write on "le tableau".
Their teacher is "le professeur",
Who sits at "le bureau"
And teaches them what they know.
Some people speak in Italian,
Others speak in Greek,
Some people speak in Spanish,
But French is what I speak.

Lorraine Delesanti
6-217

From "Prall on Parade," Anning S. Prall Jr. H. S. Yearbook, Staten Island, N.Y

Figure 7-11

listening to records, writing to pen pals, seeing films, eating in foreign restaurants, and even preparing foreign foods all add to the pleasurable experiences the child can derive from the foreign language class.

To teach the culture of the "mother country," you may assign research projects, "take trips" (imaginary, of course), introduce the great art of the nation, play recordings of its classical music, study its famous people, read books about it, and invite guest speakers to discuss it.

To make the learning fun, we have outlined activities such as playing "Simon says" and other word games, and holding vocabulary bees; making tape recordings; decorating your classroom with signs, posters, and trinkets; having the children perform short plays; constructing picture dictionaries; publishing a foreign language newspaper.

You may wish to have the children teach their families to hold short conversations in the foreign language; then invite the parents to the class, and to see films in the language. Should you decide to go to a foreign restaurant, or actually prepare a foreign dinner, they would certainly be involved.

By utilizing these experiences, you can encourage every child to participate actively, which will lead to his success in learning a foreign language.

··· 8 ···

Art, Music, and Health Education in the Experiential Manner

~~~~~~~~~~~~~~~~~~~~~~~~~~~~

We are considering, in this chapter, three subject areas which enable you to give a great many opportunities for achievement, successful achievement, to your children. Art, music, and health education all are fields in which you can bring out some talent from almost every child. Not only can you bring it out, but you can help it to flourish. Furthermore, you need not have a great deal of talent yourself to teach each of these subjects effectively. Creativity must be encouraged by setting up the situation for it to develop. Essentially it is pointing the children in the right direction, placing them on the right track, and watching them go. While not everyone will produce a work of art, or become an athlete of Olympic capabilities, you will find many doing things you never would have expected of them. Your tasks are to initiate projects, give the children simple instructions, encourage their work as they progress, and then, when it is finished, exhibit as much of it as possible. It has been said that the poorer student will excel in these subjects. We have found that, very often, this is true. Most important, every child, boy or girl, must be given feelings of accomplishment, and these are the areas where it is feasible and relatively easy for you to do this frequently. A child may not be able to read well, but if he draws a bird flying over a meadow—who is to say it is not beautiful, particularly in this era of nonobjective art?

Repeating,

1. Introduce your projects—in art, music, or health education. Motivate the lesson, of course. We believe that many of the projects you will find in this book are *almost* self-motivating because they are experiential in nature, but they still need to be approached by you with verve and enthusiasm.

179

2. Instruct your children in the methods they will need to carry the projects out. For example, you cannot hand a child a piece of charcoal, without explaining how it is used. Make the explanation brief and start the children working.

3. Walk around the room, comment, assist—but, above all—encourage. If a child cannot do a handstand, but is trying, acknowledge this. When he does it, praise him. If he suddenly plays a line of music correctly, smile and pat him on the back. Every living thing, even plants and animals, and certainly humans, thrive on attention and encouragement.

4. Exhibit work. Your room can easily become a veritable art gallery. Art is relatively simple to exhibit. But you can exhibit musical and athletic talents too, by arranging for the children to give performances in the assembly or in the gymnasium, for their schoolmates and for their parents. Those performances are important because they give many children, who are not academically talented, other opportunities to "shine."

RELATE THE CHILD'S EXPERIENCES IN SCHOOL WITH HIS LIFE OUTSIDE

Our son came home from elementary school one day and announced, "I won't learn to dance. We have dancing as part of health education, but I won't learn."

"But, Henry, you have to learn."

"I won't. I hate it. I won't."

"But Henry, dancing is so important. And it's fun, too. You'll enjoy it, once you know how."

"I don't care. I won't learn."

"I think you're closing your mind to something, and you'll regret it later on."

"No, I won't."

"But, can't you give it a try? Can't you at least make an attempt? By the way, what dance are you learning?"

"The minuet."

Doesn't that little anecdote make the point most adequately?

If a child does not see the value in what he is learning, he will not learn. If, on the other hand, the experiences you offer him are relative to his life, are things he can recognize the use for, you will see an entirely different reaction. He may not always be eager to learn, but many, many times he will be.

180

DEVELOP TASTES FOR MUSIC AND ART

Let us consider, too, engendering in your children a taste for music and art. This was called, in previous years, music and art appreciation.

Surely both art and music should be taught from the appreciative aspect as well as the creative. Surely each affects the other, but both are needed if the child is to become a well-rounded individual. Isn't every child entitled to be introduced to the "finer things in life?" A child from the slums can be stirred by a magnificent piano concerto as readily as one from an affluent family. Recognizing a Van Gogh painting can thrill a slow learner as much as a brighter child. Art and music both hold appeal for many individuals, regardless of their IQ's. Why not for our students?

Show a first grader a colorful Chagall reproduction, and he or she usually smiles happily. Play *Peter and the Wolf* and he or she beams. By such simple introductions, followed by short discussions, you whet the child's appetite. For a number of years both art and music appreciation courses have been left for the college level. Our younger children are thereby missing a great deal, for some of them will respond to the experiences we have mentioned, with much joy.

Hang reproductions of famous paintings in your room—and label each. You will find when you change the paintings, your children will come up to you, asking "Where is that bridge?" (At Arles) "Did that artist like to go to the circus?" (Dufy). Then, when they see other works by these painters, they are like old, familiar friends. The same is true of the child fortunate enough to hear "good music"—Tchaikovsky, for example, has written many beautiful melodic symphonies. Boys and girls thrill to the William Tell *Overture*, or to Beethoven's *Fifth Symphony*. Choose melodies they can hum, music they will enjoy, and you can give some of the children an interest in music which may last all of their lives.

In the same way that having flowers and plants around the room feeds a child's esthetic sense and his love of nature, so you can provide a musical background. You may play recordings while an art lesson is in progress, or while a child is doing manual work. In this way, the child who has a natural love of music will find he is emotionally nourished, while in the other children there might be awakened a feeling for music that might otherwise have gone undeveloped. The selections must be deftly and astutely made—find the tunes of worth that will be appealing. After you have played several selections, ask the children which ones they prefer, and build a program on these preferences. In this way, you can help the boys and girls develop interests which can stand by them throughout their lives.

Inexpensive reproductions of Rembrandt's *Golden Helmet*, or the work of the Impressionists, of Winslow Homer, and of modern painters such as Klee, Picasso, or Matisse will make your classroom a colorful, interesting place in which to be.

Getting Children to Create

In many schools one can see rows upon rows of bunnies or snow-flakes, Santas or daffodils, depending on the season of the year. These are often cut out by the teacher and colored by the children. We

Official Photograph—Board of Education, City of N.Y

Figure 8-1

182

suggest before you do this with your young children you ask them to create a picture first, relevant to the holiday or the topic. Then, after they have drawn or tried to create something, you can permit those who wish, to work on the stencilled materials. *But,* be sure you exhibit both types of work—and as many examples as possible.

You can help the youngsters create a picture by telling a story. For instance, many of them know Peter Rabbit—but if you tell them a story about his sister Penny Rabbit, your pictures may be a bit more original. Putting Penny Rabbit in a potentially peculiar predicament puts more ideas in their heads, and putting Peter and Penny with penguins, pussycats, and puppies teaches phonics as well.

Creating Work in the Style of Other Civilizations and Other Nations

Children are often fascinated by the art of other nations. By showing them samples and pictures of primitive art, Polynesian or Indian, and suggesting they use the style, but modify it to suit themselves, they can produce interesting work. Mexican art is colorful, as is Haitian. Even the style of ancient Egypt is fun to work with.

This method is useful if you wish to integrate social studies or language arts work with art. The American Indian's patterns can be the basis for many beautiful designs, as can the Eskimo's. The Hawaiian use of color and flowers, particularly the red and white, ginger, and the yellow and orange of the plumary, will inspire decorations which will make your children and visitors happy as they enter your room.

Modeling

Those children talented in sculpture are indeed fortunate. Help them to discover their talents by using a variety of materials. The most inexpensive can be made using newspapers; called papier mache, it is easily worked, and large figures can be made which can subsequently be painted and decorated. We have seen adorable animals, mythical as well as realistic, made in this manner, and flowers as well.

Clay, and a mixture of flour and salt and water, colored with food coloring, are good media. Encourage your children to make smaller figures with these. Remember, though, that realism is not essential, and that it is the effort made and pleasure the child and viewer receive, which are important.

Research, Then Create

You can very effectively combine research with art. If you introduce a topic, tell the children a bit about it, and then have them do some research; when they work on it, they will have more interest as a result of their research. We have seen this done with excellent results—on such varied topics as stained glass windows, styles of lettering, fashion design, and even masks.

An assignment of this kind can be used to enrich the curriculum, for you will find some interested children who will put a great deal of time and effort into it.

Again, the tie-in with social studies is obvious. But you might use

Official Photograph—Board of Education, City of N.Y

Figure 8-2

184

one with language arts as well—researching, for example, the clothing worn during the time of Romeo and Juliet or of Ali Baba. Even with science, designs such as found on butterfly wings or leaves, honeycombs, clouds, a snowflake, may prove to make interesting designs.

Murals

If you can devote a larger space, and wish to have it colorfully decorated, consider using a mural. Allow three or four children to paint on one large sheet of heavy paper. Consider such topics as the following:

> Welcome back to school (September).
> Americans All.
> Faraway Places.
> Winter Sports.
> Summer Sports.
> Spring Sports.
> Our Town.
> Street scenes in London, Paris, Rome.

To serve as an inspiration, show the children pictures of famous murals such as those of Diego Rivera. They may use a series of small or medium-sized scenes, or try to incorporate their ideas into one large picture.

You may wish to use a movie or play as a basis for a mural. Research should be done to achieve a certain amount of accuracy. "Camelot" or "Man of La Mancha" could serve as stimulating subjects.

Integrating Art with Other Subject Areas

Artwork can be very effectively integrated with almost every other part of the curriculum. Poster making, for example, is appropriate for every subject area. Specifically, in connection with reading, for example, children may illustrate books or stories they have read, or works they have written. They may draw stage settings or actual scenery for plays. The procedures may be reversed, and they may do abstract paintings, and then write compositions about these paintings.

Scenes illustrating historical events, or even scientific ones, may be attempted, as well. Designs using compasses are fun, and we've found children enjoy creating them.

Trips to Inspire

Trips taken to zoos, airports, piers, or cities can inspire compositions or drawings, poems or paintings. So can a walk in the snow, or in the woods, or on a windy day. If you, with your words, help to paint pictures in the minds of the children, they can often put them on paper.

It's a Mod, Mod World

We are living in a most colorful era. Let your children share in the bright pinks, yellows, and greens, and in the flower and rainbow designs. They enjoy drawing or painting them, and the results can provide a very cheerful classroom. We suggest you use some of the posters or works of Peter Max as guides.

Stage Sets

If you plan to do an assembly program, by selecting it early in the year, you can give your children the experience of preparing stage sets. These can be painted by attaching paper to screens, and then painting this, or by preparing frames for canvas or poster or newsprint paper. Projects of this type can provide opportunities for research as well.

Montages and Collages

These art forms are simple for the child who is not talented as far as drawing or painting is concerned. By using pictures cut from magazines or old books and arranging them and pasting them on poster paper, interesting and attractive montages can be created. Be sure the children select topics in which they are interested—sports, or clothes, flowers or cars, to name a few. Collages use objects—such as beads or seeds, yarns, macaroni, beans, dried flowers, leaves, buttons, and almost anything you can think of. Encourage the children to seek new and original media. Again, a topic or subject should be selected first, and the work created to express it. Greeting card montages and collages are fun, and a good use for old birthday, Christmas, Hanukkah, or Valentine cards.

Making Greeting Cards

Attractive greeting cards are easily made. A sheet of paper is folded in four, a booklet created, and a design drawn or painted, or even a montage or collage placed on the front page. For example, we saw a very unusual card with a figure of a boy fishing, cut from colorful cancelled postage stamps.

The sentiments may be expressed very simply, or with short poems. If young children prepare them, the parents are usually absolutely delighted, particularly for Mother's and Father's Day.

Science Fiction—Twenty-First Century—Here We Come!

Assign to your children, sixth grade or above, the designing of cars, planes, houses, or cities of the future. Or, permit them to draw Martians or Moon Men, mythical plants or animals. Perhaps you would like to use photographs of modern cities or buildings, or sportscars or planes to give them ideas. Help and encourage them to allow their imaginations to wander far and wide.

Responding to Music with Art

Play two recordings—one classical and one rock and roll, and have your children draw or paint pictures to express their responses to these types of music.

Posters

If you wish to make your classwork in lettering, and drawing, too, more interesting, consider posters and poster contests. By having your children make posters which have some valuable idea to communicate, by displaying as many as possible, and by encouraging good work, you can accomplish many things. Include humor, too, for a message may sometimes be better remembered because of the manner in which it is conveyed.

187

You may wish to use any of the following themes; these will fit into almost any class or school situation:

> Keep our school beautiful.
> Keep our neighborhood beautiful.
> Keep our town beautiful.
> Follow the rules when you play the game.
> Every litter bit hurts.
> Peace and brotherhood.

In running contests, be prepared to give the winners recognition. A gold seal, with a piece of blue ribbon easily becomes a "Blue Ribbon" when you print the appropriate words, "First Prize," on it. There may be first, second, or third prizes given each time you have a contest. But be sure you exhibit the posters, in a prominent place, as well.

Trips to Museums and/or Galleries

When you take your class to an art exhibit, explain to them what the artist's intentions were, and what he was trying to express. Then have your children try to determine whether he was successful. The Impressionists, for example, experimented with light—trying to catch an impression at any given moment. Rembrandt, too, used what we think of as an invisible spotlight on the subject of his painting.

The children will, of course, see the works of many artists, but these are for their perusal—encourage them to try to remember the names of those artists they particularly liked, so that you can discuss their work with them. Don't talk about more than one painter at a time; for this will tend to confuse the children.

Drawing Children

Have the class select one of its members to serve as a model. Alternate children, and allow everyone to draw this model. Remember, the drawings do not have to be photographic in quality, but encourage the children to try to capture the characteristics of the model, and his mood—strength, humor, vivacity, and intelligence.

You may wish to designate one or two boys and girls to be "Teachers-of-the-day." These children then are consulted by their classmates

188

—when they need paint, crayons, paper, or the like. This frees the teacher to walk around the room, assisting the children with their artwork. It is also an excellent way of rewarding good behavior, and should be indicated in the youngster's grade, thereby crediting him for the service.

MUSIC

Music is the most marvelous method to spread joy throughout your classroom. It can be used to make almost every child feel gay and happy, but far too often it is an unpleasant experience for both the teacher and the children. Girls will often sing dutifully; the boys will mouth words, but no sound comes out. Why should this be true? The techniques which follow will help make your time for music a pleasant one—fun for adult and child alike. They may even make the young gentlemen participate, but we offer no guarantees for this.

Choose Songs of Worth the Children Know and Like

Any program will be more successful if you start with familiar songs, and then progress to new selections. But choose songs with appeal for children. There is no reason that we see for avoiding the use of currently popular songs. Some of the classics are fine, of course, but working with college songs raises the spirits, while ballads generally do not. Songs such as "Ta-Ra-Ra-Boom-De-Ay" or "I've Been Working on the Railroad," "The Italian Street Song" or "For He's a Jolly Good Fellow" will encourage your older children to let themselves go—musically speaking. For the younger ones, why not try "How Much Is That Doggie in the Window?" "Happy Talk," or "Three Blind Mice?" Whatever music your children take to, and seem to enjoy should be the foundation of your curriculum. Think of how much the children love to sing "Jingle Bells," and try to find similar happy songs for the entire year.

Boys and girls often enjoy singing folk songs—both of our own nation and of foreign lands. Here, too, we suggest you choose songs with gaiety and emotion, songs which may be sung as rounds or "barbershop quartets." Encourage any child with a guitar to accompany the music.

The sea chanties, work songs, blues, and even ballads should be considered when you prepare the curriculum. Or you may do a unit comparing the folk songs of countries around the world.

Encourage the Use of Instruments in Your Class

Young children love to make "music" with pot covers, homemade drums—or even by banging on the desks or clapping their hands. It's a wonderful outlet for energy—and it's fun, besides. Older children, too, enjoy clapping to such songs as "Michael, Row the Boat Ashore" and other rhythmic tunes.

You may wish to teach your children to play such readily obtained instruments as the recorder or the harmonica. This, of course, makes it necessary for the children to learn to read music—but it motivates them, as well.

If there are children who wish to play the guitar or the piano to accompany the class, by all means encourage this. Ask for volunteers, however, and always give the child time to prepare—to spare him any possible embarrassment.

Have Your Children Write Their Own Songs

This may be done in a number of ways. For example, the children may want to put words to the music of other songs, or they may wish to compose both words and music. Parodies are lots of fun, but should be done with a purpose—and no one should be hurt or insulted by them.

Reading Music

While teaching a song, teach the words and the music simultaneously. You can, in this way, teach your children to read music.

If you wish to, you can have the children construct a paper keyboard, and "play" it—as the forerunner of the use of the piano. We have a niece who started playing the piano in this way.

If a child has a toy piano, encourage him to bring it to school. This will delight both him and the other children.

You May Wish to Play Recordings, and Then Have the Children Sing Along with the Artist

First you can play an album and allow the children to select the songs they wish to sing. Then play it again, and put the words to the songs on the board, so that the children can copy and learn them. You may have the youngsters bring in the albums, or you may supply them, but give the children the chance to listen to the songs and select the ones they like.

Many public libraries have record albums which you may borrow for this.

Arrange Performances—for All of the Children

Because performing for an audience offers a great deal of satisfaction to the children, we suggest you work out a program for your

Official Photograph—Board of Education, City of N.Y

Figure 8-3

191

class. If there are children who can perform as soloists, use them, but use, also, a chorus of your children so that the entire class takes part. To hold the attention of the audience, again we suggest you select pieces of worthwhile music with which your audience is familiar.

Acting out the songs and having dances accompanying them will make the performances more lavish. Another device you may wish to try is this: have the children paint designs on slides for use in your overhead projector, and project these as the music is being sung. This may be used very effectively too, to accompany a band or orchestral concert.

Introduce Your Children to the Music of the East

The music of India and of the Orient is very different from our own. You can play a record of Ravi Shankar, for example, to illustrate the former. Explain to the children that this music must be listened to many times before the ear becomes appreciative of it. One's first reaction may be changed considerably as one learns to love it. The tonal system, because it is unlike ours, may sound strange. Encourage the children to keep their minds and their hearts open, and learn to enjoy new experiences.

Using Props to Motivate Music Lessons

Children have fun making believe. It is easy for them to make serapes with crepe paper. Perhaps you can borrow a few Mexican hats—and using these, they become mariachi singers singing "El Rancho Grande," "The Mexican Hat Dance," or "La Cucaracha."

Young children often own cowboy hats and will be only too happy to bring them into school. Use these to motivate singing "Get Along Little Doggie" or "The Streets of Laredo." Sailor hats go beautifully with "Blow the Man Down" or "We Sail the Ocean Blue."

Have we seemed to ignore the girls? Not at all—for they can participate in any of the activities mentioned.

You may ask the children to form groups, select a song, and prepare a simple costume to go with it. Leis for "Aloha," picks or shovels and red work handkerchiefs for "I've Been Working on the Railroad," Indian headdresses for "One Little, Two Little, Three

Little Indians," or multicolored belts and suspenders for the Swiss, "I Am a Happy Wanderer," are some suggestions you can offer. A red, white, and blue crepe paper sash and a flag, and "America the Beautiful," a toy puppy, and "How Much Is That Doggie in the Window?", are others. Encourage the children to think of props and the songs to go with them. The selection of songs is unlimited if you succeed in getting your children to start using their imaginations.

Link Music with Social Studies

Is your class studying the geography of foreign lands? Why not link songs with this? The children can experience the music of the country through records, and can learn to sing along.

In terms of history, too, music can be linked to many different periods. Surely the boys and girls should realize the connection that the song "Yankee Doodle" had with the American Revolution. The American "Great Depression" of the 1930's would be felt a bit by the children if they were to hear or sing, "Brother Can You Spare a Dime?," and the period of slavery gave to American culture many magnificent songs and spirituals such as "Sometimes I Feel Like a Motherless Child." You may wish to play Marian Anderson's superb recording of this.

In the selection of songs to fit periods, both the teacher and the children can be very creative.

Holiday Music

Part of our heritage lies in such songs as "Over the River and Through the Wood," sung at Thanksgiving time, or "Jingle Bells" at Christmas. These songs should be sung as the holidays approach, for gaiety and spirit.

An interesting approach, too, is the use of foreign Christmas songs, sung by the entire class, or by groups of children. An assembly program called "Christmas Around the World," while not very original, is still excellent for your children. Surely such songs as "Oh Tannenbaum" have a place in their musical backgrounds.

Lullabies may be used, too, as holiday music. "Hush Little Baby" or "Suliram" are both very effective. Songs which discuss world peace are extremely important. The Hebrew, "Shalom, Havairim," or

"When Johnny Comes Marching Home Again," bring out this idea. "We Shall Overcome" is appropriate for the birthday of Dr. Martin Luther King.

Visits to Hospitals, Old Age and Nursing Homes

Senior citizens and shut-ins enjoy the visits of boys and girls tremendously. Any musical program they present would be a source of pleasure to the adults, and a wonderful lesson in compassion for the children.

HEALTH EDUCATION

Once again, we repeat the concept—*your teaching should give your children experiences which are related to their lives, and which they will use to a great extent.* For example, much stress is often placed on baseball, basketball, and track—and yet the chances of a boy playing these games in his adult life are extremely small. Instead we suggest you include, if you are able to, in your curriculum, tennis, golf, or bowling. Active participation in these sports is valuable at any time in one's life, from childhood on. In Australia many boys and girls learn tennis from first grade on. We can adapt this to our curricula—without eliminating the baseball, basketball, and track.

Encourage Participation

Boys and girls need physical activity for their muscular development and for maintenance of good health. Physicians cite, daily, the need for exercise, in terms of prevention of heart attack. Should we not have our children exercise daily, using simple calisthenics which can be done in the classroom? Our youngsters can easily jog in place, or you may wish to have them march, skip, or jump in the aisles, provided, of course, this kind of activity has not been prohibited by their physicians. Work out a number of simple activities and have the boys and girls do them each day. This procedure will help use up their excess energy and start them on the road to permanent good health. As you discuss this fitness program with them, mention the possible deleterious effects of smoking—for this subject cannot be brought up too often. You may wish to include the exercises outlined by the Royal Canadian Air Force, for these are stated in terms of age and level of achievement. There are specific exercises for physique and figure development which can benefit every child, and this may be an introduction to a program for the child's entire life.

"Field Days" and Competitions of All Kinds

Old-fashioned field days, complete with relay races, baseball games, and competitions, such as track events, are not only a source of pleasure, but can be motivating experiences as well. Done on a schoolwide basis, they are most effective—but they can also be planned by all of the teachers of one or two particular grades.

If possible, select a park which will offer you open spaces and a feeling of freedom. Make it mandatory for each child who is physically able to do so, to take part in some of the competitions—because, in every group, there are children who prefer to "watch." Yet, if the teacher can involve these children, he or she can help them conquer this inertia.

Always schedule this event well in advance, and designate an alternate date in case of rain. Combining the field day with a picnic is logical and lots of fun. This type of experience is one the children will long remember.

If your children can afford to buy clothing especially for the field day, they may wish to wear white shorts and shirts. This adds a special festive note—and an attractive one, to the proceedings. It should be done, however, only if the financial outlay is not a problem.

Plays or Dances to Music

Have your young children interpret a story through acting or dancing. For example, first graders love "Three Times Around Went the Gallant Ship" or "The Farmer in the Dell." You may wish to have the children create their own action stories, combining language arts with physical activity.

Introduce Rhythms and Dancing

By working with simple rhythms, having the children walk and clap, or move their bodies to music, you prepare the boys and girls

195

for self-expression through movement. This kind of activity, repeated, absorbs the children, and helps them "let themselves go."

As they reach the intermediate grades, they should be taught social dancing. This must, of necessity, include the dances currently popular. If you are personally unable to teach them, perhaps you can invite another teacher, a child in the class, or several children in the upper grades to do so.

We cannot stress the importance of this. We have, at dances, often seen most of the children, usually boys, lined up against the wall. Most of the time the reason is simple—they don't know how to dance. Surely they should, for dancing is a marvelous way to enjoy oneself, to utilize one's energy—and to become socially comfortable. If it is at all possible, teach them—not the minuet, but the dance of the day. There are dances which have been popular for many, many years—but the boys and girls can learn them later on. Today the twist is more important than the tango, the watusi more current than the waltz.

Be sure you have both boys and girls dancing together—for if they are taught separately, many retain their bashfulness. Dancing may tremendously enrich the children's lives—in adulthood as well as childhood—for one loses a great deal in life if one doesn't learn to dance.

Just allowing the boys and girls to dance is not enough. They need to be taught the actual steps and the movements. If you merely allow them to dance, you will find far more spectators than participators, which is exactly what we are trying to avoid.

Modern and Interpretive Dance

Modern and interpretive dancing offer a great deal of opportunity for self-expression. You can initiate these activities, with young children, by having them form large circles, and then asking, "Have you ever thought of what would happen if you were a piece of paper?" "Where would you be?" (Suggest they lie down.) Now, what would happen if a gentle breeze came along? A strong wind? (As they act out these concepts, encourage them to move their arms and legs.)

Use other bases for dancing, such as imitating a horse galloping or a puppy shaking itself after a bath.

196

You may allow the children to do the "choreography," or do it yourself, but stress freedom of movement—and allow plenty of room. In interpretive dancing, have the children aim to lose their identity and become the person or concept you wish to give life to.

Exhibitions of Skill

You may have a very unusual assembly program—which should be, but does not have to be, presented in the gymnasium. Have children do such activities as rope climbing or barrel jumping. Also work out exercise routines, to be done by the entire group in unison. These may be the physical fitness exercises discussed previously or other, more difficult activities.

Plan your program so that the most exciting exhibits of skill are performed at the very end. The human pyramid, for example, often serves as an excellent finale. It is very exciting—and, if it isn't successful, it is sure to provide a note of humor.

Square Dancing

"Square" as an adjective is usually used in a derogatory manner, but this is not true of square dancing. This activity combines skill, music, and intricate patterns—and, like social dancing, must be taught in detail. However, it can give your children many hours of pleasure.

If you have difficulty acting as a caller, it is possible the parents of some of your children can—and often they are very pleased to be invited. Square dancing may be included in the "assembly programs" described above, adding a colorful note in terms of dress and music.

Conclusion

Give your children experiences in art, music, and health education. It is imperative that these experiences be of value to them in terms of their daily lives. They should be of such a nature that they help bring out the children's talents, giving them opportunities to succeed and feel successful.

They should encourage creativity and participation on the part of each and every child.

Specific experiences in art, music, and health education can add notes of happiness and gaiety to your classroom, and can make your children more well-rounded individuals. These should then be our goals:

1. Relate our teaching to our children's lives.
2. Help them to discover and develop their talents.
3. Encourage them to do creative work.
4. Build a background, in each child, of art and music appreciation.
5. Make our classrooms gay, happy places in which to be.

Try to participate yourself. Children will enjoy their activities even more if their teacher is participating. We recall being applauded for catching the ball when we played baseball with the children, and for touching our toes while the girls were doing exercises. If we cannot draw well, but try, cannot sing, but still make the attempt, we can avoid becoming bored—but far more important, we can be good examples for our children to copy.

... **9** ...

Developing Good
Interpersonal Relationships
and Practicing Brotherhood

Of the many concepts we must teach to our children, the most important is the need for developing good interpersonal relationships with all of the people with whom one comes into contact. We may call this love of mankind or we may call it brotherhood, but it is a far stronger, more positive emotion than tolerance. Being tolerant means or implies we "put up" with another person. The feelings we hope to help you develop in each of your children are strong and definite, drawing them toward others as they understand them better.

Our survival as a nation depends on our ability to get along with other nations. Yet we must start with individuals, getting along with other individuals—for if people can't cooperate, can't live and work together, how can nations possibly do so?

We will suggest a number of techniques which you may use to teach interpersonal relationships and brotherhood. The most important is to have the children experience love from you—that you teach by example. You should arrange projects which have children working together closely. Teach the history of minority groups of all kinds, and discuss the need for brotherhood openly and frankly. You may wish to establish a library within your classroom for studying these subjects. Debates and plays, done by your children, are very valuable; utilizing movies, theatre productions, and television programs is another technique you may wish to adopt.

In this chapter we then go on to discuss the developmental patterns exhibited by children with learning problems, and try to sensitize you to their special needs. We describe hidden prejudice, and help you to detect it. You will find, too, a short listing of books to broaden your understanding. These are books which will aid in your self-scrutiny, which are thought provoking, and which you will thank us for recommending. Methods are given for handling the bigoted child, and giving him experiences to combat this bigotry. A phenomenon we call "intellectual discrimination" is described, and methods given to avoid it.

In the implementation of every activity in this chapter, your guidance is absolutely essential. You are the key person, and your attitudes will allow your children to experience brotherhood more than anything else. Think through all of these procedures, and if you wholeheartedly subscribe to them, you will be able to make them eminently successful. It is your actions which will speak louder than any words.

DEVELOPING GOOD INTERPERSONAL RELATIONSHIPS

Teaching by Example

There is a saying, "Do as I say and not as I do." But this is not the way to teach; nor is it the way to live. Teachers are still models for their children, still emulated and imitated. If you are warm and friendly to everyone, if you smile, if you put your arm around a child, and if he happens to be of another race or nationality, your pupils see you and copy your behavior. This love of people and lack of prejudice which you are showing serves as a silent sermon to them, far more eloquent than a verbal one. If you treat every child with dignity, no matter how poor he is, or what color he is, or his religion, or his degree of intelligence, your feelings will be communicated to all of your children. They will truly experience your love.

How do you treat every boy or girl with dignity? Never, for instance, by saying to any child, "You are stupid!" Instead you might say, "I'm sure you can do better than that!" Of course you can see the difference. Even if the misbehavior persists, you continue. "Why do you do such things? You are an intelligent person. You have a fine potential. Let's try to develop it." When one tells a child he is bad or stupid, the child will behave that way. Any name one calls him plants a seed in his mind. By planting a positive seed, by building up the self-esteem of the child, by giving him a feeling of individuality or self-worth, we make even the less fortunate child feel that he has dignity. When we make a child feel he is unimportant, we hurt that part of his mind which can least stand the damage. All children, and adults, too, must feel they have value to society, and therefore to themselves. A child who has developed these feelings of self-worth has an excellent chance of becoming a successful adult.

Arranging Projects

Try to arrange projects on which your children may work together. Set up committees which are integrated—not only by nationality or color, but by ideas, as well. When children do not work well together, determine the cause. Is one youngster domineering, and thereby causing the others to feel frustrated? Are there some children who are not doing their share of the work? Are there cliques within the committees, interfering with the harmonious relationships you hope to see established? After you have found the cause of the difficulty, work to eliminate it. Talk to the children, explaining the reasons for their problems. This method of having people work together helps them to get to know each other, and fosters experiences in good interpersonal relationships of a true, viable nature.

In the section on Social Studies, in Chapter 7, you will have found many projects which may be used with this concept of working together in mind.

One of the projects you may elect to have the children work on is history of the neighborhood, its inhabitants, and their countries of origins and backgrounds. Take the children on tours of the streets, or better still, have them take you and introduce you to the people of the area. Work to develop pride in the community and in its residents. You might invite graduates of the school back to speak to your children. Use any and all devices to build a feeling of pride in the youngsters.

Teaching the History of Our Minority Groups

Familiarize yourself with the history of all of our minority groups, and teach this to your children. For example, the Negro and his relationship to slavery has been taught for many, many years in our schools. His contributions, his heroic acts, his scientific discoveries, should be emphasized as well. Have you heard of Crispus Attucks, one of the first Americans to fight against the British? He was one of the first casualties of the "Boston Massacre." Or Dr. Charles

Richard Drew, the brilliant physician whose blood bank in a New York City hospital served as the model for the American Red Cross, and whose work on blood serum made him immortal? Ironically, Dr. Drew died because he was refused admission to a hospital after he had met with a serious accident.

Discussing Brotherhood Openly

Do not be reticent about discussing brotherhood and the tremendous need for it. Far too often this subject, which a teacher might consider embarrassing, is allowed to go unnoticed. As educators, it is our moral obligation to teach the disastrous effects of hate and violence. We must face the issue squarely—that anti-Semitism exists, even now; anti-Negro feeling is present in our land; liberal thinkers are suspected of being communists. The finger may be pointed at any and everyone. Were there not many adverse comments made when John Kennedy was a candidate for the Presidency—because he was a Catholic? The saying, "A chain is as strong as its weakest link," is very true today—and there seems to be so many weak links in ours!

Unless we teach ethics and a moral code, and live by these ourselves, we are being derelict in our duties, and we are not improving the world for ourselves, our children, or our grandchildren. We must try, by education, to strengthen those weak links. Here are some methods you might wish to experiment with:

1. Why not decorate your classroom with sayings such as the following:

"All men are created equal." *Declaration of Independence.*

"So that government of the people, by the people, and for the people shall not perish from the earth." A. *Lincoln.*

"Love thy neighbor as thyself." *The Bible.*

"Let us no more be true to boasted race or clan, but to our highest dream, the brotherhood of man." *Thomas Curtis Clark.*

2. Why not set up a section of your class library for the study of brotherhood? There is a plethora of information available from many of the social service organizations:

a. Anti-Defamation League, B'Nai B'Rith, 515 Madison Avenue, New York, N. Y.

b. Institute of Human Relations, 165 East 56th St., N.Y.C.

c. National Committee Against Discrimination in Housing, 35 West 32nd St., New York.

d. United States Government Printing Office, Washington, D.C., publishes a vast amount of material on many subjects. Write to them for a listing of publications.

e. American Friends Service Committee (Quakers) Community Relations Program, 160 North 15th Street, Philadelphia 2, Pa.

f. National Association for the Advancement of Colored People, 20 West 40th Street, New York 18, N. Y.

When you build this library, be sure to include materials which will interest the children—rather than adult publications, dull looking, and difficult to read.

3. Panel discussions, debates, plays, open discussion—all will prove very effective in teaching the ideals of brotherhood. Free and open dialogue, referred to by some as a "speak-out," is particularly good within the confines of the classroom.

Dramatizing incidents from literature or history, or from the experiences of your students, in this area, can provide entertainment as well as present a message. Your ingenuity, your resourcefulness, your efforts are badly needed in this area.

4. Assembly programs are an excellent means of inculcating the ideals of good interpersonal relations and brotherhood. One of the authors did a series of plays in the lower grades; for example, one was a modern version of the traditional Cinderella theme. She and the children converted it into a musical which rang with songs composed by the pupils and their teacher. Here is one, called, "The Prince's Birthday Ball."

Oh, let us come and dance with joy
My subjects brave and free.
I care not what your race or creed
Or what your color may be.
Jew and Christian, white and Negro, beloved subjects all,
Forever welcome in our land, and at my birthday ball.

So sang the prince of this new Cinderella. The next stanza was sung by a chorus, representing the prince's subjects.

Oh, let us come and dance with joy
It is our prince's day.
He opens wide his heart to us
To us, his subjects gay.
Jew and Christian, white and Negro, beloved subjects all,
Forever welcome in our land, and at his birthday ball.

It was a veritable ball too, because the mothers had made beautiful costumes, and had, of course, been invited to share in the triumph of the production. The words remained (inscribed in beautiful lettering), on charts which decorated the classroom for many, many years. It was hoped the ideals were so inscribed in the children's hearts.

It has been said that one picture is worth a thousand words. Why not fill your school—halls, offices, bulletin boards with cartoons and pictures which the students have made, and which are apropos to the magnificent idea of brotherhood? How proud they will be when they see them displayed—their own brain-children.

Can we utilize movies and plays in this area? Of course! Take your classes to see such films as "The Heat of the Night," "Guess Who's Coming to Dinner," or "The Two of Us," which are enjoyable as well as educational. Very often the television screen offers such wonderfully enlightening films as "A Gentleman's Agreement." Be sure they are called to your pupils' attention.

FIGHTING BIGOTRY

Our Own Reactions

Do we react in the same manner toward all children? Have we special feelings in regard to the slow learner? Many of these children are to be found in groups which have not learned the mores of most Americans, which are out of the "mainstream," and which require a great deal of work in the field of acculturation. As scientists look for cause and effect relationships, so should we. The expression, "The sins of the fathers are visited upon the children," is no more applicable under any circumstances than it is in the case of education. The background a child receives before he even enters the door of a school varies tremendously. There are many children who are lacking in the fundamental communication skills, and because they have difficulty in expressing themselves, may become frustrated, and consequently angry. This frustration proves to be their, and our, worst enemy. These are the children who, most often, develop learning difficulties.

Then, as their school lives progress, they meet this enemy—this frustration, again and again. How do you think you would react? Remember, you have probably never in your life experienced this constant sense of a failure. It is the slow child you especially must help, for he needs your help; but he may react by seeing you as the cause of his lack of success.

Consider the child who never does his work. Why doesn't he do it?

Is it because he simply can't? The disruptive one—the caller out—the nasty child—why is he that way? Is this his lack of success screaming at us?

We must, every single teacher, every counselor, every supervisor, every person involved in education, take a long look at our views, our ideas, our deepest convictions, for we hold, actually hold, the future of human beings in our hands. We decide, in our everyday world, which children will grow up to succeed, which will be doomed to failure. We prepare our youth for jobs or for indolence. We build their self-image—to contribute to society, to be a burden upon it, or even to be a menace to it.

Question yourself. Does a child's color make a difference to you? Does the slant of his eye have influence on you? Does his speech pattern or a foreign accent make you see him in a different light? Or are all children equal in your eyes, regardless of their origin? Must we not treat each child as a precious individual—placed in our care, under our tutelage, each child, whom Longfellow referred to as a "living poem"?

Personality Clashes or Prejudice?

No teacher will ever get along perfectly with every child. Nor will every boy or girl love every other boy or girl with whom he comes into contact. Personality clashes are real and do exist, but their significance is based on the reasons for them. If Jimmy annoys you because he makes snide remarks—that's a personality clash. If he irritates you because he is of a different color, nationality, or religion, then your reaction is a manifestation of a very serious character defect, which you must consciously work to overcome. And you can overcome it if you analyze your reactions to people and study them. Psychoanalysts tell us that if one is aware of his problem, he has taken the first step toward the solution.

There should be no place in the classroom for the prejudiced person, and should you encounter such feelings, we hope you will try to counteract them. The battle must be an unending one, because, unfortunately, there are far too many who have drunk bigotry in with the milk at their mothers' breasts.

We have heard of one teacher who told her children, "You wouldn't want any of 'them' in your class, would you?" And true to the adage, "A little child shall lead them," it was a child who complained to his father because he was upset by the remark. "Them" referred to the children of another race. The child's father became irate, and brought the matter to the attention of the principal who took action against the teacher.

We know of one librarian who refused to allow poor children to borrow books from the library because they would "dirty them and spoil them." A teacher overheard this comment and repeated the remarks to his supervisor. The librarian is no longer in that school, because, although various people in authority spoke to her, she refused to change her attitude.

The most incredible part of these stories is that the individuals did not realize they were prejudiced. When confronted with it, they denied it vehemently. Psychologists tell us that each person has some prejudices, and it is for this reason we say the fight against bigotry must be a never ending one, and we, the educators, must be in the forefront of the battle.

Sensitivity to Almost Hidden Prejudices

Have you ever heard the remark, "What can you expect of *him?*" Why, why, why? Why should we not expect the most of every child? Our feelings toward other groups make themselves known in many ways. A boy told us he had bought his watch, which we had admired, in "Jewtown." In some areas it is considered highly humorous to discuss Polish janitors, Italian garbagemen, Chinese laundrymen, Irish drunks. Why do we, after 200 years, still mention the national origin of people? Aren't all of these individuals now Americans? These remarks are truly misleading, for our country is beautiful because of the many nationalities and races represented here.

Not all human beings are aware of the wounds others may suffer because of their callousness. One of the authors read a newspaper column consisting of the humor of an Italian comedian who, although he had changed his name, used a great many anti-Italian stories. She wrote a letter, which was published in the local newspaper, complaining about the image given to young Americans whose parents had come from Italy. A number of people thanked her for writing the letter, but there were others who believed the humor to be very funny, and asked "What are you so sensitive about?"

Please, our colleagues, be sensitive—for the psyche of every child with whom you come into contact. The child called a "Dirty Jew" suffers traumas which may, and probably will, remain with him all of his life. The Negro child has, in the few short years of his experience, been slighted not once, but many, many times. There is no such thing as being a slow learner when it comes to learning about prejudice. If you have not read Sammy Davis Jr.'s book, *Yes I Can*, we cannot suggest too strongly that you do so. It will give you a great deal of enlightenment and insight into the lot of the American Negro. All of us desperately need this enlightenment, and incidentally, and very importantly, we need it whether we teach Negro or white children.

There are many parts of our nation where white American children have never had any close contact with Negroes, children or adults— but they have heard stories, and have been given stereotypes, for many years of their lives. It is our task to show them that all people are alike, regardless of race or color; that we have the same hopes, dreams, ambitions; that we have the same variations in personality, in ability, in temperament, whether we descend from the original colonists, from the Indians who preceded them, or from the immigrants who later came to our shores. When a person lives with different kinds of people, works with them, and becomes friends with them, his out-look changes. But, for those living in areas which are so stable that the ethnic background of the inhabitants have not changed for many years, our task, to help these people to understand and feel compassion for others, is of paramount importance.

Suggested Readings for the Teacher

Other books we suggest you read are John Howard Griffin's *Black Like Me*, Moynihan and Glaser's, *Beyond the Melting Pot*, Ross and Hill's *Employment, Race, and Poverty*, and a most exceptional textbook, *Behavior and Misbehavior*, by James Hymes, Jr., published by Prentice-Hall, Inc. in 1955. The latter should be a must for every teacher. It is a great book!

Each of these books will contribute to your understanding of the problems facing the minority groups today. We must realize that our school situation is a great leveler. Sitting before us may be a child who has had a sleepless night because his apartment is infested by rats. (We had the experience of having a child fall asleep in class!

When we questioned him, he gave this reason. How can a teacher chastise a child for this—and yet, how is she supposed to have known the reason for his behavior?) You may have, in your class, children whose paternal parents have never been seen, and others whose fathers beat them. You may have children who have felt the cold fingers of the death of a loved one, or who never, ever, knew the warmth of their mother's kiss. The era of mass production has made it possible for even those youngsters whose families are getting public assistance to be well dressed. You rarely know each child's story, but you must realize that many children can and do have severe problems in their home lives. (More often than not there is such a story to be found in the background of some of your children.)

We must warn you to remember, too, never to reveal a child's story inadvertently. Many times children are released from mental institutions and returned to school. This information is highly confidential; depending on the school's policy, it may or may not be revealed to the teachers. The reason for this is a very important one. We once heard a teacher tell a child, "If you don't behave yourself, you'll go right back into .... State Hospital." The teacher realized what an error he had made because the entire class gasped. Of course, the child did not conform to the school requirements—partially, one might suppose, because of the comment, and the fact that all of his classmates knew what should have been his "secret." He was returned to the confines of the institution. How different the pattern might have been, had the teacher been discreet. This is an unusual anecdote, however, because most of us are professional, and would not perpetrate such outrages, even unthinkingly. However, we must be aware of the various backgrounds and the difficulties many children have, although we do not discuss them.

Handling the Bigoted Child

What would you do should you discover a child who refused to work with another child because of a color difference? Would you accept this behavior, or would you try to work with both children? Would you be afraid to discuss the matter in class? Good teaching, you know, requires courage and conviction. You must have both. Arranging projects on which the children work together is one particularly good way to break down barriers. Set up your groupings

210

carefully, and make sure you give them adequate supervision. Working with individuals or groups of children by talking with them, explaining to them the need for cooperation, showing them that all people have a great many things in common, will help to change the bigoted child. Discussing bigotry in class, too, is important, for by a frank and open discussion, you can bring out fears and problems which might be "swept under the rug" otherwise. It is not enough for you to be relatively unprejudiced, you must teach your students, too, to fight bigotry.

Bigotry is one of the scourges of life. It is a national shame, for it is accompanied by poverty and corruption. And, as teachers, we must be brothers to all of mankind. We must teach our children to live together, or, to paraphrase Ben Franklin, we shall all assuredly die together.

Intellectual Discrimination

An insidious type of discrimination is often practiced, yet the persons, if accused, would be dumbfounded if you confronted them with it. They would say, incredulously, as children so often do, "Who, me? Never!" But they are, or may be, guilty of demanding too little—of saying, "That's all that child can do," and letting it go at that. The child then goes through life impoverished by neglect, unintentional neglect. Don't allow yourself to fall into this pattern. All of your children, but particularly your slow learners—rich or poor, white or Negro, Jew or gentile, good or bad—need all of the help you are able and willing to give them.

Let us trace the development of a child experiencing difficulty in reading in the first grade. He manages to comprehend about 50 per cent of the work. "That's all he's capable of," Miss Smith thinks. "I can't help him!" But Miss Smith, you can! And you must! Because, assuming you do not, by second grade that child is doing considerably less than 50 per cent, and by the fourth grade he is probably retarded two or three years in his reading.

Every boy or girl should be encouraged to try harder. And the more skillful a teacher you are, the more he or she will try. He or she makes the attempt for many reasons. You might say, "I'm sure you can do better. Let's see how I can help you." Or, you may say, "Dear, we're going to find out what it is you are having trouble with, and, once that is cleared up, I'm sure you will progress very rapidly." *If you determine where the difficulty is, and work on it—you can usually help the child to improve.* Conversely, if you stop trying, so will the child.

We've attributed many characteristics and qualities to teachers; that you need the patience of a saint is not being said lightly. You simply must have it, as every teacher must. Have you ever encountered, as we have, a delightful little seventh-grade girl who cannot subtract— the result of intellectual discrimination? Isn't it amazing? A child has been taught by teachers for six years, and still cannot perform this fundamental skill. Perhaps some teacher she may yet find will be able to lift the veil from her eyes in the field of mathematics.

As the children enter your classes, give them diagnostic work to find out what their learning problems are, and once having found them, work with the children to eliminate their difficulties. Don't allow yourself even to think, "This is the best Sally can do." The song, "The Impossible Dream," says it well—that nothing is impossible. As teachers we must not only believe this philosophy, but we must live it.

In the upper grades, by demanding good work from each child in your classes, you do far more than the teacher who will accept anything, regardless of its quality. If you assign a report, for example, teach your pupils how to write it. Let us suggest some procedures for you to follow (these may be used in any subject area):

1. Choose a topic of interest to your class.

2. Outline slowly, clearly, and carefully the manner in which you would like your pupils to proceed.

3. Show them where and how to get their information. Is it from reference books or their text? Tell them where to find it.

4. Show them examples of reports well done. You may distribute rexographed samples if you wish.

5. If the work would be improved by charts or drawings, teach them how to do them. Here, too, samples are important.

6. If a bibliography is to be included, teach the class exactly how to do one.

7. Have each child put a cover on his report. Supply construction paper for it.

It is essential that you check on the work as the children progress. Give helpful hints, encouragement, and actual assistance when necessary. Do not accept work of poor quality, even if the project must be rewritten once, twice, or three times. You will discover that the next assignment you give will result in work of better quality.

When the work is acceptable, reward the child with a high mark, remembering we use grades as encouragement, to get each child to work up to his or her capacity. Make sure the child experiences a feeling of success. You may also display the work to further build the child's self-esteem.

Conclusion

We must work with our children to help them develop good interpersonal relationships and feelings of brotherhood. With these goals in mind, we have discussed a number of activities.

We suggested you teach "brotherhood" by actually living it, by bringing the children together while working on projects, by giving them information in regard to their various cultural backgrounds, by establishing a library for their use, by holding panel discussions, by producing assembly programs, by utilizing moving pictures and television presentations.

We are sure that you agree with us wholeheartedly that there is a deep need to fight bigotry in ourselves and in others. To accomplish this end we suggested severe self-scrutiny, so that we insure our minds and our hearts being open to any child, regardless of race, creed, color, financial standing, religion, or academic ability. Specific readings were suggested; we have tried to give you insight into the lives of children whose minds have been blighted by bigotry, and who consequently may have developed mental blocks which cause them to be stigmatized as slow or reluctant learners.

Teachers often demand too little of the slow learner. We have termed this "intellectual discrimination," and urge you to be wary of it. When a teacher says, "What can you expect of Joe?" or Sally, Bill, or Mary, what he is really saying is, "I can't teach this child." Please do not allow yourself to fall into this trap. Work with each child until

Official Photograph—Board of Education, City of N.Y

Figure 9-1

he does learn. Each of us must make a commitment—to the children we are privileged to teach—that we will do all we can to help each boy or girl reach his potential, and that we will not be satisfied with a minimum amount of achievement.

The classroom is the cradle of learning, where good interpersonal relations and the brotherhood of man must be taught again and again, if we, our children, and humanity are to survive.

···10···

Questioning to Make
Learning Experiential

Although most schools do not have courses in wood carving, this skill is practiced by many, many students. One example is often found on classroom desks,

"DEDICATED TO THOSE
WHO DIED WAITING FOR THE BELL."

How much of our children's intellect dies each day—how much of their curiosity, their creativity, their interest dies—waiting for that signal which signifies the end of the period or day? And what of those boys and girls who simply "turn off" the teacher—who do not hear his or her voice—and who consequently do not have any idea of what activities are taking place in the classroom. Some children, if they find the instruction dull, may take refuge in flights of fancy; others in exciting matters such as the latest baseball score; the unsocial child in misbehavior; the troubled child in attention-getting devices; the adolescent in romantic daydreaming; and the slow learner in any or all of these. How can we, in our classrooms, avoid these situations? The answer, we believe, to this very important question, is so simple! Question, don't lecture. Questioning is an integral part of the experiential learning program.

It is our belief that many teachers are not aware of the fact that they are lecturing. We have pointed this out, and found them to be quite surprised by our observations. We believe that many fine teachers lecture because they are not aware of the need for other, more effective methods. The last four or more years of their lives as students were spent in colleges, where the instruction consists almost entirely of lectures, and this carries over into their daily work. We hope to show you how your teaching will be far more effective on any level if, instead of lecturing to the children, you encourage them to tell you as much as they can. Questioning provides for an interchange of ideas and a stimulation of thought. We believe it to be an art, a skill which can be developed. For example, let us consider this sentence presented to a class in language arts. "The man, who lives in the house next door, has a dog." Some teachers might say, "This sentence has four nouns—man, house, door, dog." Would it not be preferable to say, "This sentence has four nouns. Who can tell us what they are?" Which way would you phrase it? You can learn about your own teaching with a bit of introspection. Perhaps you would like to tape one of your own lessons to see just how much of the talking you do. Are you a lecturer? If so, maybe you will decide to change your technique as you read on.

Almost every time you make a statement, follow it with a question. "It looks as if it's going to snow. Has anyone heard the weather forecast?"

This is spontaneous—it is almost a manner of speech, which you can develop. However, you should seed your lesson plans with questions, so that you do not have to think them up on the spot. You should prepare questions, in advance, which will be geared to the intellectual levels of all of the children, encouraging everyone to participate.

With rapid-fire questioning techniques, you stimulate the children and "keep them hopping." Thoughts flow through the air as a result of this. If you relate the questions to the children's lives, they will have less difficulty in responding to them. If the questions are dramatic or humorous, they will add to everyone's enjoyment. Don't be afraid to do this. It's excellent teaching! Above all, do everything to foster curiosity on the part of the reluctant learner, as well as the better student. If it were possible to psychoanalyze many of our slow learners, we are sure they would prove to be children whose natural curiosity was stifled at an early age. Shouldn't you try to rekindle it—by getting the children to ask questions—and by asking them yourself as you teach? If the climate in the classroom is one of give and take, the children will feel free to speak, and to question as well.

QUESTIONING PROVIDES AN INTELLECTUAL GIVE AND TAKE

By employing skillful questioning, you can draw all the children into the lesson. Start with easy questions, but do not permit the bright children to usurp the lesson by giving most of the answers.

By directing these easy questions to the slow learners, they are able to actively participate. If the questions are too difficult, they withdraw. As the lesson proceeds, make the questions more challenging to the bright children. If your opening questions are above the heads of the reluctant learners, they will lose interest in the lesson immediately, and it will be less than valueless to them, for it will make them feel inferior. This, in turn, may cause them to become disruptive in their behavior. If, on the other hand, they are drawn deftly into the lesson, by directing your questions first towards them and enticing their interest, they feel at home in the classroom, their learning can be improved, and their behavior is less likely to be objectionable. In the lower grades, the following pattern will illustrate the track to pursue:

"Who has a little brother or sister at home? Have you a little brother or sister at home.....Jim?"

"I have a sister."

"How old is she?"

"Three."

"What's her name?"

"Alice."

"Did she ever meet with an accident, or come near being hurt?"

"Once she touched the stove and burned her finger."

"Tell us what happened—do you remember just what she did?"

And here you have the beginning of a valuable safety lesson. By skillful and imaginative questioning, ideas are often generated that may later be developed into a safety play, written by the children, in which the slow learner could be cast in an important role. Whether or not his performance is adequate is relatively unimportant. What is important is that he does not become the forgotten child, either in his own mind or in the mind of his teacher. Incidentally, we have often been surprised by what the slow children can do. Our yardsticks for measuring their abilities are far from perfect.

Probably the most important indication of successful teaching is the vitality one feels as the class progresses. We can acquire this vitality by a give and take with all of the children, rather than by conducting a monologue or dialogue with the brighter members of the class.

Who among us has never been subjected to the classic bore at a dinner party—the one who talks, and talks, and talks, and usually says nothing of value? Socially, do we not enjoy meeting the person who seeks our opinions, who listens with respect, and who is genuinely interested in people and their problems? In the same way, we should be interested in our little people and their little and big problems. We can structure our classes to avoid being boring by learning to be skillful questioners. One of the most eminent dental educators, Dr. Samuel Charles Miller, maintained that any lecture longer than 15 minutes was a complete waste of time. Don't you agree?

DEVELOPING THE ART

The art of questioning, and it really is an art, requires development; one doesn't learn to draw out information immediately. For example, after the teacher has decided what concepts he wishes to cover, he frames questions which will do this. In teaching a lesson in science on an eighth-grade level, let us consider the topic, "Humidity." The teacher, to motivate the lesson, should not ask, "What is humidity?", but, "Why do we say, 'It's not the heat—it's the humidity' during the summer?" From this question he might draw out the actual meaning of humidity. This might be followed by, "Perhaps you have heard the statement. 'The relative humidity is 90 per cent.' Whose relatives? Your aunt Mildred or your little cousins Alice, Jimmy, and Frank?" A discussion of relative humidity would then ensue. Next he might ask, "What does humidity look like?", or "When do we experience its effects?", or "Why are we more conscious of it in the summer?" In using this method of presentation of material, you, the teacher, must determine the ideas you want your children to learn, but, instead of saying, "Smog is a mixture of fog and smoke," you ask, "Who has heard of smog?" "What is smog?" "Under what circumstances does it form?" (You might also ask, "What's snew?" As we have previously stated, humor is always a welcome addition to any classroom situation. "What's snew? Nothing. What's new with you?".)

Use your questions to reach every child. Call on volunteers some of the time, but by no means at all times. You may find that questioning a child who is inattentive will bring him back into the lesson, if he has been "wool-gathering." If he doesn't know the answer, say to him, "That's all right, Bill. I'll give you another chance later in the lesson." This almost forces him to participate. In the elementary grades, as a rule of thumb, every child should be called on at least once each day. If you work toward this goal, all of your children will benefit. It is so easy to fall into a pattern of calling on the hand-wavers constantly. But remember, this will have disastrous effects upon the self-images of the other children. Try to direct your questions to every one of them!

What does questioning accomplish? It passes the intellectual ball back and forth, between the boys and girls and the teacher, and, better still, between the children and their classmates. The slow learner may be caught up in this exchange as well as the normal or brighter child, and, almost before he is aware of it, is participating. To most successfully use this technique, work out your most important questions when you write up your lesson plans. How, why, when, where are far better than questions requiring a yes-no answer. You may make a statement and ask the students if they agree with it, and if so, why. If not, of course, why not? In developing a lesson in this way, you aim for understanding rather than for rote learning.

KEEP THE QUESTIONING MOVING RAPIDLY

In order to keep your questioning moving rapidly, you must stifle the impulse many of us have to repeat the children's answers. If repetition is necessary, ask the child answering or another child to give the response again.

When you have developed your concepts with the children, write them on the board or have a student do so. Any material covered should be written as well as discussed. This is essential, for, as we have said previously, some of the children take very poor notes unless the material is written for them.

If it is necessary for you to give your children facts, which they have not contributed themselves, relate them to the material you have previously discussed. For example, the following is a lesson or lessons on the Pure Food and Drug Acts.

Motivation

Show photographs of children born to German mothers who had been taking the drug Thalidomide. How did these tragedies happen and why?

If your children possibly recall it, have them tell you what they remember of the case. Be sure that they understand the cause-and-effect relationship. For example, ask the following questions:

(a) How did doctors determine that the Thalidomide caused the birth defects?

(b) Why didn't we have any women in this country taking the drug? It was recommended by many physicians in Germany, for example.

(c) How many of you know who Dr. Frances Kelsey is? She received the nation's highest honor for federal employees. (Dr. Kelsey is, of course, the medical officer working for the U.S. Food and Drug Administration who became alarmed by reports concerning the drug, and prevented it from being made available to people in our country.)

Then say to your class, "We will now go on to learn about the way in which our government works to protect us from harmful foods, drugs, and cosmetics. What is the name of the agency which never ceases to look after us?"

Now, instead of presenting factual material, here are some of the questions the teacher should ask to bring out the facts:

1. The first Federal Pure Food and Drug Acts were passed in 1907. What do you think they were? (You should try to get from your pupils the concept that these first laws dealt with only interstate and foreign commerce in food and drugs.)

2. Why were they necessary? (Now you want the children to tell you of the dangers of impure foods and of meat which was handled very badly in the meat-packing plants.)

3. Has anyone read or heard of Upton Sinclair? Who was he? What was the effect of the publication of the book *The Jungle*? (If no one is able to answer the questions, read several paragraphs aloud. Be careful to select particularly stimulating ones. Then ask for volunteers to read the book and report back to the class.)

4. What do our more recent laws do? (You are trying to bring out the idea that they protect public health, prevent fraud in the sale of food and drugs, and cosmetics as well. They also forbid the sale of foods, drugs, and cosmetics which do not show on the label the exact content of the product.) After each item, you should ask, "Why is this important?"

5. What do we call a person who buys products? (This is a relatively poor question because it has a one-word answer, but use it to introduce the field of consumer education.)

224

6. Why is the testing of drugs and foods very important to everyone? (Refer to your motivational photographs.)

7. How are violators of these laws punished? (Fines from $1,000 to $10,000. Manufacturers or shippers found guilty of breaking the law may also be imprisoned from one to three years.)

8. What federal department do you think is in charge of enforcing the Pure Food and Drug Acts? How do they do this?

9. Does anyone in your family belong to an organization called Consumers' Union? (You would try to find a child who is familiar with the organization and its work. If there is no one in the class, request a volunteer to go to the library and bring back issues of the reports and of the yearbook.)

10. In what way does our government seek to protect us from cigarettes? (Ask a child to bring in an empty cigarette pack from home, never one from his or her pocket.) Have the child read aloud the warning printed on the package. Discuss this at length.

11. How do the cigarette companies try to get us to buy their products? (You might want to include some material on the psychology of advertising.)

Your purpose in questioning is to stimulate thought, enliven your teaching, encourage your children to reason and work along with you. Obtaining and maintaining their participation is worthy of your most strenuous efforts.

RELATING YOUR QUESTIONS TO YOUR CHILDREN'S LIVES

Referring to our previous lesson, many, indeed most, of our pupils have been subjected to television commercials from the time they were two years old, and possibly even younger. Ask them, for example, if they recall September and the fall season of toy advertising on TV. Why are toys advertised in the fall?

By referring to such concepts, based on previous learnings, you can draw the child into the lesson and make him eager to contribute. Children love testing things, too, and doing this in the classroom will please and interest them.

When you phrase your questions, make sure you indicate the name of the child after pausing at the end of the question. For example, "Why is a law such as the Pure Food and Drug Law necessary?" (Long pause.) "Mary? Janet?" If at least half of the students aren't volunteering, you may prod them with, "Who can see what might occur if we didn't have it?" After waiting, call on a child who has not spoken during the course of the day.

Never say, "Jane, why is this law needed?" The reason is simple; once you mention the name, the challenge is limited to the one child you are questioning. It is pedagogically poor and may even indicate favoritism; the other boys and girls might feel slighted.

Try to avoid calling repeatedly on the same children. Perhaps you will find it necessary to make your questions simpler to reach all of your pupils. If need be, do so. For example, if you asked, "Why do you think cosmetics were added to the laws regarding pure food and drugs?" and only a few hands were raised, you might add, "How are cosmetics related to drugs?" or "Can cosmetics harm anyone?"

Make yourself consciously aware of the procedures you follow. Use a variety of questions, so that you are sure every child in your group will be intellectually challenged. It is possible to ask one question which brings forth many replies, and you may be able to move from child to child, asking, "What do you think?" This is good because of the feeling of a current passing through the group. How thrilling it is to electrify children with ideas! Try such a query, as, "How far can our government go to try to stop people from smoking?" Or an even more basic concept is brought out when you ask, "Why shouldn't people smoke?" Every child should be able to express some opinion in regard to these things. Nod your head after each response, and call on as many boys and girls as have answers. Your object is to get your material from all of your children and keep your lesson moving.

Encourage the pupils to ask questions, about anything which interests them, or about which they are curious. Get their contributions whenever possible; have them answer each other's questions. If a child asks a question which is at all relevant, seek answers to it. If the question must be tabled, do not forget to return to it as the lesson progresses. But, above all, keep the lesson moving! Prevent every child from becoming bored.

Questioning effectively is a skill, one of many which comprise the art of teaching. Your adeptness will improve if you consciously train yourself to use this method. It is an art which will flourish if you seek to develop it.

We have watched a teacher who is the mother of a young child talking to the little one. She said, "Do you see the bird? What color is the bird?" After the child responded, she said, "Yes, he is yellow. He's a canary. Can you say canary?" The child repeated the word, and then she said, "Good! What color is a canary?" The questioning technique had become so much a part of her way of speaking that she used it to educate her own baby.

Train your children to look for relationships between facts, concepts, ideas. Get them to think about practical applications. For instance, after doing a lesson on graphs, you might ask the class, "What events in your own lives might we plot on graphs?" Each child might chart his grades; the daily temperatures; the amount of time it takes to read a certain number of pages; the amount of time spent watching television. Then ask questions to give them practice in reading the graphs.

DRAMATIZE YOUR QUESTIONS

In certain lessons, dramatizing the subject matter by your questions will stress the important details. For instance, "Why do you never turn on the light while you are in the bathtub—if you love life?" Or, "During a storm, if a wire is torn down, and is lying on the ground, why must you keep far away from it—far, far away?" Another query, "If you are swimming and a sudden storm comes up, why must you get out of the water?" Or, "Your neighbor's basement is flooded, and he starts to pump out the water. Sudden death! Why?"

Water is an excellent conductor of electricity—so much so it can easily kill a human being—in the bathtub, in the streets, in a swimming pool, and in a flooded basement. You must get this concept across to every child, if you are teaching science, social studies, language arts, or even mathematics. Questioning will help you do it, and your pupils will remember the warnings far longer than if you stood in front of the class saying, "Now remember, if it starts to rain, get out of the pool. Electric current is conducted by water and you could be electrocuted."

In trying to keep the pace of the lesson moving, do not skip from question to question too quickly. Give the students time to think of the answer or answers to the problems you are posing. If you try to get about two-thirds of the students to raise their hands, you probably have waited long enough.

Both the homework and the warm-up, too, can stimulate a give-and-take as the children state their responses, and each corrects his own work.

You will find that when teaching you must draw children out; indeed you must almost literally pull them into your lessons. I recently substituted for a teacher, and it required almost 30 minutes for me to show the pupils they were capable of answering my questions. The topic was the introduction of the Civil War.

I started this lesson by asking, "Who knows what the Civil War is called in the South?" Not one volunteer.

I tried again. "You know no one in any southern state refers to a Civil War. What do they call it?" Still no response.

It was disconcerting to see a sea of blank faces—uninterested, almost lethargic. "How many of you have heard of the war between the states?" Six hands went up.

"What was the war between the states?" Four hands remained up. Timidly the response came, "The Civil War?"

"Good for you," I responded, heartily. The boy smiled. One of the others commented (without bothering to raise his hand) "That's easy."

Silence again. The teacher whose place I had taken obviously had good control—too good. The pupils were afraid to open their mouths. "Anyone come from the South?" I asked. Three hands went up. "Where?"

Two boys were from North Carolina, one girl from Alabama. "Do you like New York better?" Two did, one didn't. "Why?" (Anything to get them to respond.) "It's too cold here." (This from the girl from Alabama.) Far afield from the lesson? Absolutely! But, anything to get some participation, some life into the class. Then I had an idea, "Did you see the article about students' clothes in the last issue of our school paper?" (This referred to a column asking the principal for permission for girls to wear mini-skirts, and for boys to be permitted long hair and boots.) "What would happen if everyone decided to wear what he or she wanted?" I asked. "Would that be a Civil War?" That did it. The floodgate opened. The discussion flowed, became heated. Children were shouting out. I called for order—but, when it was over, the youngsters had come out of their shells. "Why couldn't we have a Civil War? Right here in school?" The children themselves realized the need for leaders and rules, even if everyone didn't agree with them. Worthwhile? When they see me in the halls, these pupils grin and say, "When are we going to have a Civil War in school?" It's become a joke—a bond between us. But the thrill of seeing lethargic children come to life, become animated, interested—isn't that what we look for in this work? And it was the questioning that triggered it. Not the information I gave them—but what they told each other.

STIMULATING YOUR CHILDREN'S NATURAL CURIOSITY

Children have natural curiosity which so often is crushed instead of nurtured in school. We remember seeing a vignette on the bus. A lady and her little girl (about four years old) sat down in front of a dignified old gentleman. The child asked her mother, "Why do the cars ride near the bus?" "Where are these people going?" "What time is it?" "Where are we now?" She kept asking—one question after another. Finally, the mother, in desperation, said, "Darling, please. No more questions for a little while."

The dignified elder leaned over, "Madam," he said, "That is no way to bring up children. You must answer their questions. You aren't helping your little daughter to grow up properly."

"Perhaps you're right," the mother answered. "What is it you just asked me, dear?" And the dialogue continued.

Fifteen minutes later, as our friendly advisor prepared to get off the bus, he leaned over again, "Madam," he said, "I don't blame you a bit—"

What do we do in school to kill their curiosity? Must we not constantly nurture it? And can we not, by our own questioning, even bring out their curiosity? When children feel comfortable, and are intellectually stimulated, the thoughts and the questions flow. It is our job to make this happen.

We have heard a child ask a difficult, really thought-provoking question, and have heard the teacher answer, "That is a very good question. Look up the answer for homework." You won't catch that youngster asking questions about anything as long as he remembers the first incident! When children ask questions, they want answers. Of course, it may happen that you don't know the answer. Involve the entire class, ask for volunteers, or do the research yourself—but don't punish the child for asking. We all want immediate gratification, to some extent. Therefore, try to get the information from the rest of the class. You may be surprised at how often you can do this. If you are able to supply it, do so; if not, look it up yourself.

We are reminded of the little boy who asked his father, "Dad, in new math, what is a set?" "Gee, son, I can't help you with that. I don't know new math at all." A bit later he returned, "Dad, in science, we're learning about ionization." "Sorry, Billy, I never had that when I went to school." Then, again the boy was stumped. "Dad, where is Dien Bien Phu?" "Let me see. I've heard of it. Can't quite recall, but I'll try. Maybe you better look it up." Once more the child needed help, so he approached his father again—again to ask him something. But he changed his mind, turned away. The father saw this, called to him, "Son, what is it?" "Oh, never mind, Dad." "No, no, son, what is it? You know, if you don't ask questions, how are you ever going to learn?"

Might that not be a good motto to paraphrase for ourselves—if *we* don't ask questions, how are they ever going to learn? How is the child to participate—without questions? How is he going to escape from the trap of not being able to read well? How is he going to learn of new, fascinating, interesting things? Through questioning!

TESTING

Surely a logical outgrowth of "questioning" is a discussion of testing. While we believe teachers must give tests, we do not subscribe to the "once-a-week, every-Friday" concept. Tests should be given at the end of a unit of work, to determine whether or not the children have grasped the material on which you and they have been working. If you have been including questions in your planning, these will now stand you in good stead, for the thought-provoking questions you have asked throughout the unit should surely be repeated in your testing.

Since we believe reasoning is far more important than the recall of facts, essay questions must be included on every test you give. The question which starts with the words, "how" or "why" is very important in showing you the extent of a child's understanding. He also should learn to handle such questions—for they are asked of him repeatedly—throughout his school and adult life. If a child does not know how to answer an essay question effectively, he is at a decided disadvantage. Train your children to analyze essay questions, to determine what information is called for, and then the manner in which to supply it most satisfactorily.

Let us say your tests will consist of the following:

> 50%—essay questions
> 50%—other types of questions

The latter category may include any or all of these:

True or False:

A question such as "The capitals of New York, New Jersey, California, and Colorado are Albany, Trenton, Sacramento, and Denver" is better than "The capital of California is Sacramento."

True or Change the False Statement to Make It True:

The U.S.S. *Titanic* was sunk when it collided with another ship.

Multiple Choice:

Match the words in column A with the meanings in B.

( ) condense   1. a pipe
( ) convene   2. to oppose
( ) concrete   3. to declare to be wrong
( ) condemn   4. to get together
( ) confront   5. a mixture of cement and sand
( ) conduit
( ) convoy

Note: there are more items in one column than the other.

Multiple Choice:

Richard Nixon, John Nance Garner, Lyndon Johnson, and Aaron Burr were *all*: (a) Presidents of the United States; (b) Vice-Presidents of the United States; (c) both President and Vice-President; (d) neither President nor Vice-President of the United States.

Completion:

"Beware the Ides of March" is from a play by ....

By our illustrations we have tried to show how all of the short-answer questions asked would require some reasoning.

Whenever you give a test, allot time to go over it carefully with the class. After it has been corrected, if it is not discussed, dissected, and even fought over, it loses much of its value.

Just giving a child a numerical grade, but not allowing him to see his paper, is both a waste of time, and of one of our best teaching tools. The test questions themselves can serve as powerful stimuli to learn. Every paper should be returned to its author, gone over in detail, and the incorrect responses corrected and learned. In this way, the test has value. Omitting this negates much of that value.

Another use, for the teacher, of tests, is to see how much of the material many of the children have not grasped. If a question is missed, it should be retaught. If most or even a third of the children have not been able to answer the questions correctly, the topic should be covered again, with the entire class. In this way, the test serves as a diagnostic tool for the teacher.

We have heard of tests which were failed by three-fourths of the class. This is an indication that the material was not presented well, and certainly was not learned by the children, or that the questions were inappropriate. It is absurd to penalize them for this. Should this occur in your class, repeat the work, after questioning the pupils orally to determine what, specifically, they did not understand. What if every child gets a perfect score? You may look at this in two ways: the material is too easy or the children really learned this work. If the former is true, a purpose is still served. Every child is given a feeling of satisfaction. Therefore, don't disregard the test. Make the next one a bit more difficult—but not too much so. Those feelings of achievement are tremendously important.

An interesting device you may decide to try is to have the children submit questions. Tell them they will be writing their own test, but that they are not to make it too easy. Instruct each child to submit a specific type of question, one which he feels is vital and germane to the work the class has been studying. Then, when you actually compile the test, use as many questions as possible.

There are many educators who do not believe testing has value. We feel that, since tests are, like death and taxes, inevitable, we should give our children experiences in test taking. Academic success is impossible without developing the ability to do reasonably well on tests. Essay answering is particularly important, and essays should be included in every test you give.

Conclusion

Please answer the following questions without reference to the chapter. No need to write them—mentally or aloud will be fine:

- How does teaching on the elementary or secondary level differ from the college level?
- Why do we need to question constantly?
- How can you develop the art of asking good questions?
- Why do children need this type of teaching?
- Which types of questions may be fired at children? Which require more time?
- How can you relate your questions to your children's lives?
- Why is the expression used, "Questioning is an art."?
- How can you ask dramatic questions? Why bother?
- What can you do to foster the children's natural curiosity?
- How can you use the questions you prepare each day as a means of review?
- Why should you be sure your children are capable of answering essay questions?
- Have you answered these questions? Wasn't this more valuable for you personally than reading a "conclusion"?

Some Concluding Thoughts

In the words of Jean Jacques Rousseau, "To live is not merely to breathe, it is to act, it is to make use of our organs, senses, faculties, of all those parts of ourselves which give us the feeling of existence. The man who has lived longest is not the man who has counted most years, but he who has enjoyed life most."

Experiential learning means that the child lives and breathes education. No longer is he confined to a little seat and desk or a single school building. Now the whole world becomes his classroom. The magnificent media of science and art can transport him to the far ends of the earth. He is no longer merely a spectator of the play enacted on our planet. He becomes an eager participant, helping to enrich human life as well as to partake of it. Let us open wide the doors of the theatre, the concert hall, the cinema, and the gates of travel. Let us nurture his creative abilities, so that he and his fellow students may enjoy to the fullest possible measure the fruits of his intellectual and spiritual powers. We, his teachers, can provide the "Open Sesame," to a new and better world for him and for humanity.

•   •   •   •   •   •   •   •

Index

A

Absentees, telephoning, 83
Acculturation, 163
Acting, 51
Alice in Wonderland, 99
Animal sounds, 93
"Annabel Lee," 108
Art:
  collages, 186-187
  colorful era, 186
  develop taste, 181-182
  drawing children, 188
  getting children to create, 181-182
  greeting cards, 187
  humor, 187
  integrated with other subject areas, 185-186
  lettering, 187
  mod, mod world, 186
  modeling, 183-184
  montages, 186-187
  murals, 185
  museums and/or galleries, 188
  of nation, 167
  posters, 187
  research, then create, 184-185
  responding to music, 187

Art: (Cont.)
  science fiction, 187
  stage sets, 186
  style of other civilizations and nations, 183
  trips to inspire, 186
Artwork, 51
Astrology, 124
Astronomical observatories, 128
Atomic energy plants, 128
Audio-visual aids, 156-157
  (*see also* Social studies)
Authority figure, 22
Automation, 40

B

Banks, operating, 130
Bees, 48
Behavior and Misbehavior, 209
Beyond the Melting Pot, 209
Bigotry, fighting:
  handling bigoted child, 210-211
  hidden prejudices, 208-209
  intellectual discrimination, 211-212
  our reactions, 206-207
  personality clashes, 207-208
  suggested readings, 209-210

Moving pictures:
  language arts, 108
  various subject areas, 42
Multiple choice questions, 231
Murals, 52, 185
Music:
  develop taste, 181-182
  East, 192
  encourage children to make "music," 190
  folk, 151
  have children write songs, 190
  holidays, 193-194
  hospitals, old age and nursing homes, 194
  link with social studies, 193
  performances for all children, 191-192
  play recordings, 191
  plays or dances for health education, 195
  props to motivate lessons, 192-193
  reading, 190
  responding with art, 187
  rhythms and dancing for health education, 195-196
  sing along, 191
  songs with appeal for children, 189-190
Musical plays, 112

N

Narcotics, 127
News broadcasts, 110
Newspapers:
  class, 44
  foreign languages, 167
  social studies, 148
Newspaper office, 108
Notebook, 54
"Notebook Completion Week," 70
Notes, copying, 54

O

Old Yeller, 99
"Open End," 111

Open-end stories, 98
Opinion polls, 149-150
Outermost House, 128
Overhead projector, 156
Overtime work, 45-46

P

Parties, celebrity, 150-151
Pen pals, 162-163
Personal stories, 47
"Pets," 69
Photography, 125
Picture dictionaries:
  foreign languages, 165-166
  reading and language arts, 102-103
Planetariums, 42-43
  (see also Trips)
Planting, doing for school, 123
Plants, 122-123
Playlets:
  foreign language, 164-165
  on-the-spot, 29, 51-52, 94-95
Plays:
  old ones in modern dress, 52
  reading, 99
  reading and language arts, 112
  safety, 108
  to music, 195
Poetry lesson, 108
Political campaigns, 110
Population figures, 134-135
Posters:
  foreign languages, 170-171
  making, 185-186, 187
Prejudice, 201-215
  (see also Interpersonal relationships)
President of class, duties, 80
"Primal sanities," 22
Problems, handling:
  approach, 65
  closeness with children, 65-66
  cooperation of children, 69
  effectiveness of truth, 69
  "notebook completion week," 70
  relate school to world of work, 67

MURIEL SCHOENBRUN KARLIN has taught children in elementary and junior high school, acted as educational and vocational counselor, and has been active in teacher training for years. She is now an assistant principal in a New York City junior high school, and is conducting a special workshop for teachers. She has taught teachers in the Summer Institute for Teachers of the Disadvantaged, and is the author of many articles in educational journals, and is co-author of *"Successful Methods for Teaching the Slow Learner."*

REGINA BERGER taught for many years in the New York City school system. She is particularly interested in finding avenues of approach to teaching children of diverse backgrounds and abilities, and has originated many experiential methods presented here. As in the case of this handbook, she co-authored the widely used *"Successful Methods for Teaching the Slow Learner"* with Mrs. Karlin. Miss Berger has also written poems and short stories.

Developed in that crucible of teaching children with diverse backgrounds and abilities, the New York City School System, here is a program for making children WANT to learn.

A program of motivational learning experiences that relate study not to abstract concepts, but to children's everyday needs and interests, it totally involves them in the learning process.

By calling for the active participation of ALL the children—the slow and the bright, the timid and the bold—it transforms the whole class as if by magic. It puts an end to apathy and the disruptive behavior that apathy breeds.

The Handbook enables you to turn lessons your pupils may consider as humdrum into adventures in learning. Instead of coming to class with reluctance, they will come because it is an exciting place in which to be.

To begin with, it shows how to *prepare* the children for learning experiences. It shows, for example:

- **How to make them WANT to learn to read (so they can follow the printed instructions for building a model airplane or a radio, for sewing a dress or baking a cake).**

- **How to make them WANT to learn to write (so they can send for free tickets to a radio or television broadcast).**

- **How to make them WANT to learn the multiplication table (so they can take part in a classroom competition similar to a spelling bee).**

- **How to make them WANT to learn mathematics (so they can figure out**